COME FOR Tea

COME FOR *Tea*

Favorite Recipes for Scones,
Savories, and Sweets

Hoffman Media
1900 International Park Drive, Suite 50
Birmingham, Alabama 35243
hoffmanmedia.com

ISBN # 978-1-940772-89-9
Printed in China

ON THE COVER:
(Front Cover) From "Celebrating Mothers,"
pages 43–54.
(Back Cover) Lavender, Mango & Peach
Macarons, page 117

Contents

Introduction

IT HAS BEEN SAID THAT THE WORDS "come for tea" are among the most pleasing anyone, especially a tea lover, could ever hear or read. Whether printed as a formal invitation on pretty stationery, sent as an email, or uttered in a telephone conversation, a request to join someone for tea is a delight.

While it is always marvelous to be the recipient of such an invitation, it can be equally rewarding to host family and friends for teatime, especially for a special occasion. Five menus and table settings for the holidays most celebrated with afternoon tea—Valentine's Day, Easter, Mother's Day, Thanksgiving, and Christmas—grace the pages of this tome. Sections with à la carte recipes for scones, savories, and sweets follow, providing additional options. All foods featured are sized to work well on most tiered stands. While the classic arrangement is to have all three courses on one stand, you'll see in these pages various presentations that provide a twist on tradition. Award-winning author and tea educator Jane Pettigrew said it so well, "It is the personal choices and individual creative touches to the tiered stand that make teatime such a timeless pleasure."

Novice hosts may find the concepts we present in "Tips for Hosting a Tea Party" (page 10) to be quite helpful, and our "Tea-Steeping Guide" (page 14) instructs on best practices for preparing a great pot of tea. The tea pairings for every menu have been expertly curated so that the infusions you serve work well with the fare and theme. Whenever possible, recipes include make-ahead tips for food preparation to minimize stress the day of the party. And if you're concerned about entertaining guests who have gluten sensitivities, you'll find the index on page 134 to be a valuable reference, as it highlights recipes that are completely gluten-free.

Whatever the occasion, we hope you will treat yourself and others to a meaningful celebration as you invite them to come for tea.

TIPS FOR *Hosting a* TEA PARTY

EXTENDING INVITATIONS

Formal invitations are a lovely and thoughtful way to communicate the details of the upcoming event, as well as to be sure you have an accurate count of those who will attend. Although invitations printed or written by hand and mailed are certainly preferred, technology has made it acceptable to extend them via telephone or email. Invitations should include the following information:

• Date and time of the event (between 2:00 and 5:00 p.m., with 4:00 p.m. being preferred.)

• Address of venue

• Name of host(s)

• Information and deadline for RSVP

• Preferred attire (Specify only if clothing should be more formal or more casual than usual for afternoon tea.)

CREATING YOUR OWN MENU

Whether planning treats for two or a large crowd, putting together a menu for an afternoon tea can be a bit daunting if you've never done that before. Typically, one flavor of scone, three savory options, and three sweet offerings will fill most tiered stands and are manageable to prepare. By following our tips for each of these categories, you can create teatime menus that delight your guests and that will allow you to enjoy their company as well.

Scones—Some hostesses and tearoom owners choose to serve scones as a first course because, as they point out, scones are best hot out of the oven. Others prefer scones as the second course, in which case, they either place these breads on the corresponding tier of the stand to be eaten at room temperature or bring the warm scones to the table only at the appropriate time.

If scones are petite, allow two per person; otherwise, one each should be sufficient. Select a flavor and a shape that will be compatible with the other courses and with the selected theme. Choose condiments that complement the taste of the scone, and be sure to allow enough for each guest, serving them in personal portions in petite bowls, such as antique salt cellars, or in containers that will hold enough for all of those seated at the table.

Savories—Offer your guests three different options to enjoy for this course. While tea sandwiches are traditional favorites, consider incorporating savory tartlets, miniature quiches, and other flavorful bite-size items into the menu. Coordinate flavors, textures, and shapes with the tea-party theme. To avoid last-minute stress, opt for recipes that can be made ahead, at least in part, or that require minimum preparation time.

Sweets—Because this course traditionally sits in the place of honor on the top tier of the stand—or might even have an entire stand dedicated to it—and is the last to be eaten, incorporating a variety of shapes, flavors, textures, and colors here is quite important. Three sweets of different types will make the final installment of the tea menu interesting and memorable. Keep the portions small, especially if the treats are rich.

Embellishments—Fresh fruits, herb sprigs, and edible flowers can be colorful fillers for any tiered stand. Grapes, strawberries, raspberries, and orange wedges are popular choices. Star-fruit slices, kiwi slices, kumquats, and currants are less traditional but add wonderful shapes and flavors. Fruit slices that turn brown easily, such as apple and pear, should be tossed in citrus juice before using. Garnish trays with herbs and flowers that are pesticide free and food safe. Mint, rosemary, sage, and thyme are attractive, fragrant options. Roses, pansies, marigolds, violas, primroses, and orchids are excellent choices. We recommend growing your own flowers or buying from a reputable source, such as Gourmet Sweet Botanicals (*gourmetsweetbotanicals.com* or 800-931-7530).

PREPARING THE FOOD

Tea fare is usually best made à la minute, or just before serving. Unless you have a lot of help in the kitchen, it is often logistically impossible to wait until the day of the event to prepare the food. Many of the recipes in this book include a "MAKE-AHEAD TIP" section, but general tips for making favorite teatime fare in advance follow.

Scones—Freeze raw scones on parchment-lined baking sheets. Once frozen, transfer scones to airtight containers or bags, and store in the freezer for up to a month. Just before serving, place desired quantity of frozen scones (do not thaw) on parchment-lined baking sheets, and bake in a preheated oven according to recipe, allowing an additional 5 to 10 minutes for adequate doneness and browning.

Tea Sandwiches—Most fillings can be made a day ahead and stored in the refrigerator. Assemble sandwiches a few hours before the tea party, drape with damp paper towels, cover well with plastic wrap, and refrigerate until needed.

IMPROVISING A THREE-TIER TRAY

If you don't have a three-tier tray for displaying scones, savories, and sweets at your next tea party, don't panic. There are clever ways to improvise this elegant serving piece.

• Stacking ceramic or glass cake plates is a possibility. Many vendors offer cake plates in graduated sizes that are perfect for this technique.

• If matching cake plates are not available, consider using similar styles but different patterns together—for example, three cut-glass cake plates of varying styles or three ceramic cake plates of different colors.

• If you have a treasured china pattern, Replacements, Ltd., the china-matching service in Greensboro, North Carolina, will make a three-tier tray for you, using three sizes of plates—usually a dinner plate, a salad plate, and a bread-and-butter plate. For more information, call 800-737-5223, or go to replacements.com.

SELECTING AND SERVING HOT TEA

When choosing the types of tea to serve, offer a choice of at least two to accompany and complement your food selections. (The menus in this book feature a tea pairing for each of the courses.) Generally, strongly scented teas should be avoided. Instead, opt for classic blends, single-origin teas, or favorite fruit-flavored infusions. Having a caffeine-free alternative is a thoughtful gesture caffeine-sensitive guests will appreciate.

• Use loose-leaf tea rather than prebagged. (See our "Tea-Steeping Guide" on page 14 for more information.)

• Make tea an hour or two ahead, and keep it hot in thermal carafes in the kitchen until ready to serve. (Do not use containers that have ever held coffee, as the lingering oils from the coffee will impart an unpleasant taste to the tea.) Because green, white, and some oolong teas are delicate, it is best to prepare them right before serving.

• In the kitchen, warm teapots with hot water, discard water, and fill teapots with hot tea from thermal carafes just before serving.

• During the party, keep the tea warm by tucking the teapots under tea cozies, which are safe alternatives to lighted tea warmers and are available in many pretty and practical designs.

TEA-STEEPING *Guide*

The quality of the tea served at afternoon tea is as important as the food and the décor. To be sure your infusion is successful every time, here are some basic guidelines to follow.

WATER

Always use the best water possible. If the water tastes good, so will your tea. Heat the water on the stove top or in an electric kettle to the desired temperature. A microwave oven is not recommended.

TEMPERATURE

Heating the water to the correct temperature is arguably one of the most important factors in making a great pot of tea. Pouring boiling water on green, white, or oolong tea leaves can result in a very unpleasant brew. Always refer to the tea purveyor's packaging for specific instructions, but in general, use 170° to 195° water for these delicate tea types. Reserve boiling (212°) water for black and puerh teas, as well as herbal and fruit tisanes.

TEAPOT

If the teapot you plan to use is delicate, warm it with hot tap water first to avert possible cracking. Discard this water before adding the tea leaves or tea bags.

TEA

Use the highest-quality tea you can afford, whether loose leaf or prepackaged in bags or sachets. Remember that these better teas can often be steeped more than once. When using loose-leaf tea, generally use 1 generous teaspoon of dry leaf per 8 ounces of water, and use an infuser basket. For a stronger infusion, add another teaspoonful or two of dry tea leaf.

TIME

As soon as the water reaches the correct temperature for the type of tea, pour it over the leaves or tea bag in the teapot, and cover the pot with a lid. Set a timer—usually 1 to 2 minutes for whites and oolongs; 2 to 3 minutes for greens; and 3 to 5 minutes for blacks, puerhs, and herbals. (Steeping tea longer than recommended can yield a bitter infusion.) When the timer goes off, remove the infuser basket or the tea bags from the teapot.

ENJOYMENT

For best flavor, serve the tea as soon as possible. Keep the beverage warm atop a lighted warmer or under your favorite tea cozy if necessary.

BE MY

Valentine

The MENU

SCONE
Cranberry-Pear Scones
🍵 *Organic Black Rose Tea*

SAVORIES
Beef Filet & Romesco Crostini
Radish Slaw Frico Cups
Creole Shrimp Salad Tea Sandwiches
🍵 *Organic Black Currant Tea*

SWEETS
Strawberry-Macadamia
Flourless Cakes with
Sour Cream Buttercream

Chocolate-Cherry Bonbons

French Macarons with
Key Lime Filling
🍵 *Organic Coconut Oolong Tea*

Tea Pairings by True Leaf Tea Co.
713-218-6300 | trueleaftea.com

Pretty pink blossoms,
dainty tea wares, and
tantalizing treats set
the scene for a beloved
afternoon tea.

Cranberry-Pear Scones

MAKES 10

Fresh pear, dried cranberries, and ground anise give these scones an unexpected, yet marvelous, flavor. Be sure to choose a ripe, firm pear, such as Bosc. And to retain the heart shape of the scones, don't skip the freezing step before baking them.

2½ cups all-purpose flour
⅓ cup plus 1 teaspoon granulated sugar, divided
1 tablespoon baking powder
½ teaspoon fine sea salt
½ teaspoon ground anise
4 tablespoons cold unsalted butter, cubed
½ cup chopped peeled, cored firm pear, blotted dry
    on paper towels
⅓ cup dried cranberries
1 cup plus 3 tablespoons cold heavy cream, divided
½ teaspoon vanilla extract
1 large egg

• Preheat oven to 375°. Line a rimmed baking sheet with parchment paper.
• In a large bowl, whisk together flour, ⅓ cup sugar, baking powder, salt, and anise. Using a pastry blender or 2 forks, cut butter into flour mixture until it resembles coarse crumbs. Add pear and cranberries, stirring gently until combined.
• In a small bowl, whisk together 1 cup plus 2 tablespoons cream and vanilla extract. Add to flour mixture, stirring until evenly moist. Working gently, bring mixture together with hands until a dough forms. (If dough seems dry and won't come together, add more cream, 1 tablespoon at a time.)
• Turn out dough onto a lightly floured surface, and knead gently until smooth by patting dough and folding it in half 4 to 5 times. Using a rolling pin, roll out dough to a ½-inch thickness. Using a 2¾-inch heart-shaped cutter dipped in flour, cut 10 scones from dough. Place scones 2 inches apart on prepared baking sheet. Freeze until firm, approximately 15 minutes.
• In a small bowl, whisk together remaining 1 tablespoon cream and egg. Brush tops of scones lightly with egg mixture and sprinkle with remaining 1 teaspoon sugar.
• Bake until edges of scones are golden brown and a wooden pick inserted in centers comes out clean, approximately 18 to 20 minutes. Serve warm.

RECOMMENDED CONDIMENTS:
Devonshire Cream
Orange Marmalade

Beef Filet & Romesco Crostini
MAKES 8

Pretty, pink slices of filet perched atop a layer of Romesco Sauce spread on a buttery crostini is a great way to say, "I love you!" But if pink isn't your loved one's favorite color for beef, then cook it to their preferred doneness.

1 (5-ounce) package beef tenderloin filet
2 teaspoons extra-virgin olive oil, divided
⅛ teaspoon garlic salt
⅛ teaspoon ground black pepper
Romesco Sauce (recipe follows)
Buttered Crostini (recipe follows)
Garnish: baby arugula, olive oil, and freshly ground
    black pepper

• Season beef filet on both sides with 1 teaspoon olive oil, garlic salt, and pepper. Let sit at room temperature for 30 minutes.
• In a small cast-iron skillet or sauté pan, heat remaining 1 teaspoon oil over medium-high heat until very hot, but not smoking. When oil shimmers, add filet. When filet begins to char, turn heat down to medium. Cook until filet is well browned. Turn filet over and cook until well browned, 3 to 5 minutes. (Filet will be rare. Increase cooking time until desired degree of doneness is reached.) Remove filet from skillet, wrap tightly in foil, and let rest for 15 minutes. If desired, for easier slicing, place wrapped filet in an airtight container and refrigerate until cold, up to 1 day in advance.
• Using a sharp serrated knife, cut filet into 8 (approximately ¼-inch-thick) slices.

• Spread an even layer of Romesco Sauce onto Buttered Crostini. Place a filet slice over Romesco Sauce, ruffling to fit.
• Garnish with baby arugula, and sprinkle with olive oil and black pepper, if desired. Serve immediately.

Romesco Sauce
MAKES ¾ CUP

Of Spanish origin, Romesco is a tomato-based sauce combined with roasted red peppers and almonds. Add some sherry vinegar, spices, and a dash of hot sauce, and this savory spread is sure to become a crowd favorite.

½ cup coarsely chopped roasted red bell pepper
¼ cup toasted slivered almonds
2 tablespoons tomato purée
1 tablespoon chopped flat-leaf parsley
1 tablespoon sherry vinegar
½ teaspoon smoked paprika
¼ teaspoon fine sea salt
⅛ teaspoon hot sauce*
⅛ teaspoon ground black pepper
2 tablespoons extra-virgin olive oil

• In a deep medium bowl, using an immersion blender, blend together roasted bell pepper, almonds, tomato purée, parsley, vinegar, paprika, salt, hot sauce, and black pepper until combined and creamy. Gradually add olive oil, blending until incorporated and emulsified. Transfer sauce to a jar with a tight-fitting lid, and refrigerate until ready to use, up to 3 days.

*We used Tabasco.

Buttered Crostini
MAKES 8

Italian for "little toasts," crostini are a wonderful bread base to enjoy with any number of toppings.

8 thin slices French baguette
1 tablespoon salted butter, softened

• Preheat oven to 350°.
• Spread a thin, even layer of butter onto baguette slices. Place slices butter side up on a rimmed baking sheet.
• Bake until butter melts and crostini are very light golden brown, approximately 5 minutes. Let cool. Use within a few hours.

- Using a sharp knife, trim and discard green tops and roots from radishes. Place radishes in the bowl of a food processor, and pulse until finely chopped. Blot chopped radishes dry on paper towels, if necessary. Store in a resealable plastic bag, and refrigerate for up to a day before using.
- In a glass jar with a screw-top lid, combine olive oil, vinegar, lemon juice, honey, sugar, salt, celery seed, and pepper, shaking vigorously until emulsified.
- In a large bowl, stir together radishes and vinaigrette until combined. Refrigerate until needed, up to 2 hours.
- Just before serving, line bottoms of Parmesan Frico Cups with lettuce leaves. Stir slaw and divide among frico cups. Serve immediately.

EDITOR'S NOTE: If left in the vinaigrette for more than a few hours, radishes will bleed and turn completely pink. For that reason, we recommend combining the radishes and the vinaigrette only within 2 hours of serving.

Parmesan Frico Cups
MAKES 6

Frico cups are not only easy to make, they're also a wonderful gluten-free alternative to bread and can hold a variety of fillings, from slaw to salad and more. To achieve the cup shape, it's best to work quickly to drape the baked cheese rounds over the backs of muffin pans or, in a pinch, shot glasses.

1 cup shredded Parmesan cheese*

- Preheat oven to 350°. Line a rimmed baking sheet with a silicone baking mat or parchment sheet.
- Sprinkle cheese in 6 (approximately 2½-inch) rounds onto prepared pan.
- Bake until cheese melts and is very light golden brown, 5 to 7 minutes. Using a metal spatula and working quickly, carefully place cheese wafers over the backs of a mini muffin pan. Let cool completely. Store in an airtight container until ready to use.

*We used packaged pre-shredded Parmesan cheese. While freshly grated Parmesan cheese can be used, the resulting frico cups will likely be more fragile and might not hold up as well to the slaw.

Radish Slaw Frico Cups
MAKES 6

Finely chopped radishes tossed in a sweetened vinaigrette replace traditional cabbage and carrots in this piquant slaw, pictured on opposite page.

1 bunch radishes with green tops
¼ cup extra-virgin olive oil
2 tablespoons white wine vinegar
½ teaspoon fresh lemon juice
½ teaspoon honey
¼ teaspoon granulated sugar
¼ teaspoon fine sea salt
⅛ teaspoon celery seed
⅛ teaspoon ground black pepper
Parmesan Frico Cups (recipe follows)
½ cup loosely packed butter lettuce leaves

Creole Shrimp Salad Tea Sandwiches
MAKES 16

Creole mustard and fresh herbs elevate this sandwich filling, making it especially well suited for a romantic or friendly Valentine's Day teatime.

1 pound large headless shrimp, peeled and deveined
1 (6-inch) rib celery
1 bay leaf
1 teaspoon fresh lemon juice*
1 tablespoon finely chopped celery
1 tablespoon finely chopped red bell pepper
¼ cup mayonnaise
3 tablespoons creole mustard
2 teaspoons chopped fresh dill
1 teaspoon fresh lemon zest*
1 teaspoon finely chopped green onion (green tops only)
¼ teaspoon fine sea salt
⅛ teaspoon ground black pepper
16 slices firm white sandwich bread, frozen
Garnish: roasted red pepper hearts**

• In a medium saucepan, cover shrimp with water. Add celery rib, bay leaf, and lemon juice. Bring to a simmer, then cover pan and turn off heat. Let poach until shrimp are pink and opaque, approximately 5 minutes. Drain shrimp and cover with crushed ice until cold. Blot chilled shrimp dry with paper towels. Place shrimp in the bowl of a food processor, and pulse until finely chopped.
• In a medium bowl, stir together chopped shrimp, chopped celery, and bell pepper until combined.
• In a small bowl, stir together mayonnaise, mustard, dill, lemon zest, green onion, salt, and pepper until combined. Add mayonnaise mixture to shrimp mixture, stirring until combined.
• Using a 2-inch round cutter, cut 32 rounds from frozen bread slices.
• Spread shrimp salad in an even layer (approximately 1 tablespoon) onto 16 bread rounds. Top each with a remaining bread round. Cover with damp paper towels and let bread thaw completely (approximately 30 minutes) before serving, or place sandwiches in a container, cover with damp paper towels, and refrigerate for a few hours until serving time.
• Just before serving, garnish with red pepper hearts, if desired.

Zest lemon before juicing it.
**Blot whole roasted red peppers dry on paper towels. Transfer to a cutting board. Using a 1-inch heart-shaped cutter, cut 16 shapes from peppers.*

MAKE-AHEAD TIP: *Creole shrimp salad can be made up to a day in advance, placed in an airtight container, and refrigerated.*

Strawberry-Macadamia Flourless Cakes
MAKES 7

Eggs, and a lot of them, are the key to the success of these decadent cakes, which sport a filling of strawberry preserves and are enrobed in a luscious buttercream.

2½ cups whole roasted salted macadamia nuts
1½ cups plus 2 tablespoons granulated sugar, divided
¼ teaspoon fine sea salt
8 large eggs, separated, room temperature
½ teaspoon vanilla extract
2 teaspoons strawberry preserves
Sour Cream Buttercream (recipe follows)
½ cup finely chopped roasted salted macadamia nuts
Garnish: 7 fresh strawberries

• Preheat oven to 350°. Line a 13x9-inch baking pan with parchment paper. Spray parchment paper only with cooking spray.
• In the work bowl of a food processor, pulse together whole macadamia nuts and 2 tablespoons sugar until fine nut particles form. (Don't over-process, or a nut butter will form!) Add salt, whisking until combined.
• In a large bowl, beat together egg yolks and remaining 1½ cups sugar with a mixer at high speed until light and fluffy, approximately 2 minutes. Add vanilla extract, beating until incorporated. With mixer at medium speed, add nut mixture to egg yolk mixture, beating until incorporated. (Batter will be very stiff.)
• In another large bowl, beat egg whites with a mixer fitted with a whisk attachment at high speed until stiff peaks form. Spoon one-third of beaten egg whites into macadamia batter, stirring vigorously to loosen mixture. Gently fold in remaining egg whites until incorporated. Using an offset spatula, spread batter into prepared pan, smoothing top to create a level surface.
• Bake until edges of cake are golden brown and a wooden pick inserted in center comes out clean, 23 to 27 minutes. (Top of cake should feel somewhat firm to the touch.) Let cake cool completely in the pan. (Due to its flourless nature, center of cake will sink, but edges will remain high.)
• Using a 2-inch round cutter and rinsing cutter between cuts, cut 14 rounds from cake, avoiding rough outer edges of cake. Using an offset spatula, transfer cake rounds to a work surface. (If cake bottoms are too sticky, place a piece of wax paper under each.)
• Spread approximately ¼ teaspoon strawberry preserves in a thin layer onto 7 cake rounds. Top with remaining 7 cake rounds. Secure layers with a wooden pick inserted in center of each cake stack.
• Using a small offset spatula, spread a thick, even layer of Sour Cream Buttercream on sides and tops of cakes. (Place remaining Sour Cream Buttercream in a covered container in the refrigerator to chill before piping scrolled design on tops of cakes.) Press chopped macadamia nuts onto sides of cakes.
• Transfer chilled Sour Cream Buttercream to a piping bag fitted with a large open-star tip (Wilton#1M) and pipe a scrolled design around top edge of cake.
• Just before serving, remove wooden picks from cakes.
• Using a sharp knife and referring to how-tos on page 130, cut "petals" into strawberries. Garnish each cake with a strawberry, if desired.

MAKE-AHEAD TIP: Cake rounds can be made up to a week in advance, stored in an airtight container with layers separated by wax paper, and frozen. Let cake rounds thaw completely before icing. Cakes can be assembled up to a day in advance, stored in a covered container, and refrigerated. Garnish just before serving.

Sour Cream Buttercream
MAKES 1½ CUPS

The tangy sour cream perfectly balances the sweetness of this amazingly delicious frosting.

8 tablespoons unsalted butter, softened
2½ cups confectioners' sugar
¼ teaspoon vanilla extract
⅛ teaspoon fine sea salt
⅓ cup sour cream

• In a medium bowl, beat together butter, sugar, vanilla extract, and salt with a mixer, starting at low speed and gradually increasing to high, until smooth, scraping down sides of bowl as needed. Add sour cream, beating until incorporated. Use immediately.

Chocolate-Cherry Bonbons

MAKES 20

Instead of a store-bought box of chocolates, serve your Valentine these homemade confections of dried cherry and white chocolate coated in bittersweet chocolate.

¼ cup plus 1 tablespoon unsalted butter,
   softened, divided
2 ounces cream cheese, softened
2¼ cups sifted confectioners' sugar
1 teaspoon fresh orange zest
½ teaspoon vanilla extract
⅛ teaspoon fine sea salt
2 tablespoons chopped dried cherries
¼ cup shaved white chocolate
1 (10-ounce) package bittersweet
   chocolate chips, melted
Garnish: dried rose petals, pink heart sprinkles,
   flaked salt, or white chocolate curls

• Line a rimmed baking sheet with wax paper.
• In a large bowl, beat together ¼ cup butter, cream cheese, confectioners' sugar, orange zest, vanilla extract, and salt with a mixer at high speed until light and fluffy.

Add cherries and white chocolate, beating until combined.
• Using a levered 2-teaspoon scoop, drop candies onto prepared baking sheet. Roll candies between palms of hands to achieve a smooth ball shape. Cover candies loosely with wax paper. Refrigerate for several hours or overnight until very firm.
• Line another rimmed baking sheet with wax paper.
• In the top of a double boiler set over simmering water, melt bittersweet chocolate chips. Add remaining 1 tablespoon butter, stirring until incorporated.
• Using a fork, dip cold candies into melted chocolate, scraping fork over rim of bowl to remove excess chocolate. Place candies onto second prepared baking sheet.
• Before chocolate hardens, garnish bonbons with dried rose petals, pink heart sprinkles, flaked salt, or white chocolate curls, if desired. Refrigerate until chocolate hardens.
• Transfer candies to decorative paper cups. Let candies come to room temperature before serving.

MAKE-AHEAD TIP: Candies can be made a few days in advance, stored in an airtight container, and refrigerated. For best texture and flavor, let candies come to room temperature before serving.

French Macarons with Key Lime Filling
MAKES 28

These classic meringue-based sandwich cookies are a light and toothsome dessert, especially with Key Lime Curd between the layers, and are best when baked on days of low humidity.

3 large egg whites, room temperature
2 cups confectioners' sugar
1 cup sifted almond meal
⅛ teaspoon fine sea salt
1 tablespoon granulated sugar
½ teaspoon vanilla extract
Pink gel food coloring
Key Lime Curd (recipe follows)

• Place egg whites in a medium bowl, and let stand at room temperature for exactly 3 hours. (Aging the egg whites in this manner is essential to creating perfect macarons.)
• Line several rimmed baking sheets with parchment paper. Using a pencil, draw 56 (1¼-inch) circles 2 inches apart onto parchment paper. Turn parchment paper over.
• In the work bowl of a food processor, pulse together confectioners' sugar, almond meal, and salt until combined.
• In the bowl of a stand mixer fitted with the whisk attachment, beat egg whites at medium-high speed until frothy. With mixer at high speed, gradually add granulated sugar and vanilla extract, beating until stiff peaks form, approximately 5 minutes. (Egg whites will be thick, creamy, and shiny.) Add food coloring, beating until desired color is achieved.
• Using a large spatula, add egg white mixture to almond mixture, folding gently until well combined and batter falls in thick ribbons.
• Transfer batter to a piping bag fitted with a medium round tip (Wilton #12). Pipe batter into drawn circles on prepared baking sheets. Tap baking sheets vigorously on counter 5 to 7 times to release air bubbles. Let stand at room temperature for 1 hour before baking to help develop the macaron's signature crisp exterior when baked. (Macarons should feel dry to the touch and should not stick to the finger.)
• Preheat oven to 300°.

• Bake, one pan at a time, until firm to the touch, 15 to 18 minutes, rotating pan every 5 minutes. Let cool completely on pans. Transfer macarons to an airtight container with layers separated by wax paper. Refrigerate until ready to fill and serve, up to 3 days.
• Place Key Lime Curd in a piping bag fitted with a medium round tip (Wilton #12). Pipe a button of curd onto flat side of 28 macarons. Top each with remaining macarons, flat side down. Push down lightly and twist so that filling spreads to edges. Serve immediately.

Key Lime Curd
MAKES 1¼ CUPS

Key lime is known for being more tart and aromatic than the larger regular lime, which makes it a bright, zesty option for a curd that can be used as a filling or spread for a myriad of pastries.

¾ cups granulated sugar
2 teaspoons fresh Key lime zest*
⅛ teaspoon salt
½ cup bottled Key lime juice**
3 large eggs
3 large egg yolks
4 tablespoons cold unsalted butter, cubed small

• In a medium saucepan, whisk together sugar, lime zest, salt, and lime juice until combined.
• In a medium bowl, whisk together eggs and egg yolks until combined. Add to lime juice mixture, whisking until combined.
• Cook mixture over medium heat, whisking constantly, until mixture thickens, 6 to 8 minutes. Remove saucepan from heat. Add butter, a few pieces at a time, whisking until incorporated.
• Using a fine-mesh sieve, strain mixture into a heat-proof bowl, pressing mixture with a rubber spatula. Cover with plastic wrap, pressing wrap directly onto curd surface. Let cool to room temperature. Transfer mixture to a jar with a tight-fitting lid, cover, and refrigerate until very cold. Use within 2 weeks.

*If Key limes are not available, regular limes can be used instead.
**We used Nellie and Joe's Key West Lime Juice.

JOYOUS
Easter

The
MENU

SCONE
Ginger, Orange &
White Chocolate Scones

Oo-Mango-Long Tea

SAVORIES
Egg Salad Baskets

Baby Pea Phyllo Cups with
Lemon-Mint Vinaigrette

Ham & Havarti Tea Sandwiches
with Roasted Asparagus

Blue Moon Tea

SWEETS
Pineapple-Coconut Cakes with
Mascarpone Cream Frosting

Almond Tea Cookies

Lemon Pavlovas

*Beatrix Potter's
Organic Herbal Tisane Blend*

Tea Pairings by Simpson & Vail
800-282-8327 | svtea.com

*A menu filled with
flavorful and whimsical
fare is befitting a jubilant
Easter Sunday tea party.*

Ginger, Orange & White Chocolate Scones
MAKES 18

Topped with a fresh orange juice glaze, this delectable scone boasts small bits of crystallized ginger as well as white chocolate chips, making it the perfect starter for an Eastertide teatime, whether accompanied by clotted cream or strawberry jam or served alone.

2½ cups all-purpose flour
⅓ cup granulated sugar
1 tablespoon baking powder
1 tablespoon fresh orange zest
½ teaspoon fine sea salt
4 tablespoons cold unsalted butter, cubed
¼ cup finely chopped crystallized ginger
½ cup white chocolate chips
1 cup cold heavy whipping cream
½ teaspoon vanilla extract
½ cup confectioner's sugar
3 to 4 teaspoons fresh orange juice

• Preheat oven to 375°. Line a rimmed baking sheet with parchment paper.
• In a large bowl, whisk together flour, sugar, baking powder, orange zest, and salt. Using a pastry blender or 2 forks, cut butter into flour mixture until it resembles coarse crumbs. Add ginger and chocolate chips, stirring until combined.
• In a small bowl, whisk together cold cream and vanilla extract until combined. Add to flour mixture, stirring just until a dough begins to form. Working gently, bring mixture together with hands until a dough forms. (If mixture seems dry and a dough won't come together, add more cream, 1 tablespoon at a time.)
• Turn out dough onto a lightly floured surface, and knead gently until smooth by patting dough and folding it in half 4 to 5 times. Using a rolling pin, roll out dough to a scant ¾-inch thickness. Using a 2-inch round cutter dipped in flour, cut 18 rounds, rerolling scraps as needed. Place scones 2 inches apart on prepared baking sheet.
• Bake until edges are golden brown and a wooden pick inserted in centers comes out clean, approximately 18 to 20 minutes. Let scones cool for 20 minutes.
• In a small bowl, whisk together confectioners' sugar and orange juice until mixture is a thin glaze. Brush over scones. Serve immediately.

RECOMMENDED CONDIMENTS:
Devonshire Cream
Strawberry Jam

Baby Pea Phyllo Cups
MAKES 12

Baby peas, or petit pois, are picked before reaching full maturity, making them sweeter than classic garden peas. Toss these legumes in a bright, citrus vinaigrette to create delectable, bite-size savories.

12 frozen mini phyllo cups
1 cup frozen baby green peas
Lemon-Mint Vinaigrette (recipe follows)
Garnish: fresh mint leaves

• Bake phyllo cups according to package directions until crisp. Let cool.
• Place frozen peas in a colander and pour boiling water over peas to defrost. Drain peas well.
• In a medium bowl, stir together peas and ¼ cup Lemon-Mint Vinaigrette until peas are coated.
• Just before serving, divide pea salad among phyllo cups. Drizzle with remaining Lemon-Mint Vinaigrette, if needed.
• Garnish with fresh mint leaves, if desired. Serve immediately.

Lemon-Mint Vinaigrette
MAKES ½ CUP

Perfect for springtime fare, this vinaigrette features the refreshing flavor of fresh mint and zesty notes of lemon, along with the sweetness from a touch of honey.

2½ tablespoons finely chopped fresh mint
½ tablespoon finely chopped fresh parsley
2 teaspoons finely minced shallot
¼ teaspoon fine sea salt
⅛ teaspoon ground black pepper
¼ cup fresh lemon juice
¼ cup extra-virgin olive oil
1 teaspoon Dijon mustard
½ teaspoon honey

• In a deep bowl, using an immersion blender, blend together mint, parsley, shallot, salt, pepper, lemon juice, olive oil, mustard, and honey until creamy. Use immediately.

MAKE-AHEAD TIP: Vinaigrette can be made a day in advance, stored in a jar with a tight-fitting lid, and refrigerated. Let come to room temperature before using, and shake vigorously to blend.

Egg Salad Baskets
MAKES 6

Cutting out wedges from hard-boiled eggs creates a whimsical basket shape that is a perfect vessel to hold a delicious egg salad.

6 extra-large hard-cooked eggs, peeled
¼ cup mayonnaise
2 tablespoons finely chopped celery
2 tablespoons dill pickle relish
1 tablespoon country Dijon mustard
⅛ teaspoon fine sea salt
⅛ teaspoon ground black pepper
Garnish: paprika and watercress

• Using a sharp paring knife, cut sliver of egg from bottom of each boiled egg so that eggs will sit level horizontally. Cut 2 wedges from each side of top half of eggs so that eggs will resemble baskets with a handle. Reserve cut pieces of eggs. Using a small spoon, gently scoop out egg yolks and add to reserved egg whites. Place egg white baskets in a covered container and refrigerate until needed.
• Using a pastry blender or 2 forks, finely chop reserved egg pieces and yolks.
• In medium bowl, stir together chopped egg, mayonnaise, celery, relish, mustard, salt, and pepper until combined. Cover and refrigerate until cold, 1 to 2 hours.
• Fill each egg white basket with egg salad.
• Garnish with a sprinkle of paprika and with watercress, if desired. Serve cold.

Ham & Havarti Tea Sandwiches
MAKES 12

Ham and cheese is a classic tea sandwich pairing. Havarti cheese offers a mildly sweet, buttery taste that nicely complements deli honey ham. For a festive presentation, garnish these tea sandwiches with a roasted asparagus half and tie with a blanched chive.

⅓ cup mayonnaise
1 tablespoon finely chopped fresh dill
1 tablespoon finely chopped fresh chives
1 teaspoon finely chopped fresh parsley
½ teaspoon fresh lemon zest
¼ teaspoon fine sea salt
⅛ teaspoon ground black pepper
1 teaspoon fresh lemon juice
8 slices potato bread
4 slices Havarti cheese
20 thin slices deli honey ham
6 stalks Roasted Asparagus (recipe follows)
12 long fresh chives

• In a small bowl, stir together mayonnaise, dill, chives, parsley, lemon zest, salt, pepper, and lemon juice until combined to make an aïoli.
• Spread a thin, even layer of aïoli onto bread slices. Top 4 bread slices each with a cheese slice and 5 ham slices, folded and ruffled to fit over cheese. Top with remaining bread slices, aïoli side down, to make 4 whole sandwiches
• Using a serrated bread knife in a gentle sawing motion, trim and discard crusts from sandwiches. Cut each sandwich into 3 equal rectangles.
• Using a sharp knife, cut Roasted Asparagus stalks to fit sandwich lengthwise, and then cut in half vertically. Lay an asparagus stalk on top of each sandwich.
• To garnish, tie a chive around each sandwich and asparagus. Trim ends to shorten. Serve immediately, or cover with damp paper towels, place in a covered container, and refrigerate until ready to serve.

KITCHEN TIP: Blanch fresh chives in hot water until pliable, approximately 5 minutes. Blot dry with paper towels.

Roasted Asparagus
MAKES 6

Asparagus tossed in olive oil, salt, and pepper before roasting for a few minutes is an easy garnish that elevates the presentation and taste of our Ham & Havarti Tea Sandwiches.

6 stalks asparagus
⅛ teaspoon olive oil
⅛ teaspoon salt
⅛ teaspoon ground black pepper

• Preheat oven to 400°.
• Place asparagus on a rimmed baking sheet. Sprinkle with olive oil, salt, and pepper.
• Bake until just tender when pierced with tip of sharp knife, approximately 5 minutes. Let cool before using as a garnish.

Pineapple-Coconut Cakes
MAKES 10

Place a layer of fruity filling between these petite coconut cake rounds, which have been cut from a 13x9-inch cake, and top them with sweet Mascarpone Cream Frosting for an appetizing flavor combination idyllic for spring.

½ cup unsalted butter, softened
¾ cup plus 1 tablespoon granulated sugar
2 large eggs
¾ teaspoon coconut extract
¼ teaspoon vanilla extra
1⅓ cups sifted cake flour
1 teaspoon baking powder
¼ teaspoon baking soda
¼ teaspoon fine sea salt
½ cup whole buttermilk
Pineapple Filling (recipe follows)
Mascarpone Cream Frosting (recipe follows)
Garnish: unsweetened coconut flakes

• Preheat oven to 350°. Spray a 13x9-inch baking pan with cooking spray. Line with parchment paper and spray again.
• In a large mixing bowl, beat together butter and sugar with a mixer at medium-high speed until light and fluffy, approximately 3 minutes. Add eggs, one at a time, beating well after each addition. Add coconut extract and vanilla extract, beating until incorporated.
• In a medium bowl, whisk together flour, baking powder, baking soda, and salt until combined. Add flour mixture to butter mixture in thirds, alternately with buttermilk, beginning and ending with flour mixture. Pour batter into prepared pan. Using an offset spatula, spread batter evenly in pan, and smooth top. Tap pan sharply on countertop to reduce air bubbles.
• Bake until a wooden pick inserted in center comes out clean, 12 to 13 minutes. Let cool in pan on a wire rack. (If cake top is not level, use a long serrated knife to make level.) Wrap cake in plastic wrap, and freeze until firm, several hours and up to a week.
• Using a 2-inch round cutter, cut 20 rounds from frozen cake, avoiding browned edges. Let cake thaw before assembling.
• Using an offset spatula, spread an even layer of Pineapple Filling onto 10 cake rounds. Top each with a remaining cake round.
• Place Mascarpone Cream Frosting in a piping bag fitted with a large open-star tip (Wilton #1M).

Pipe a rosette of frosting onto tops of cakes. Serve immediately, or place in an airtight container and refrigerate for up to a day. Let come to room temperature before serving.
• Just before serving, garnish with unsweetened coconut flakes, if desired.

Pineapple Filling
MAKES APPROXIMATELY 1 CUP

Canned crushed pineapple cooked with a few other ingredients produces a thick, curd-like filling that pairs well with sweet cake layers and would even be tasty served as a condiment for scones.

1 cup crushed pineapple with juice
¼ cup granulated sugar
1 tablespoon cornstarch
⅛ teaspoon fine sea salt
1 tablespoon unsalted butter, cut in pieces

• In a medium saucepan, stir together pineapple with juice, sugar, cornstarch, and salt until combined. Cook over medium heat, stirring constantly until mixture comes to a boil. Reduce heat, and cook at a simmer until thickened and clear, 3 to 5 minutes. Remove pan from heat. Add butter to pineapple mixture, stirring until melted and incorporated. Let mixture cool. Refrigerate until needed, up to a day.

Mascarpone Cream Frosting
MAKES APPROXIMATELY 2 CUPS

A soft and spreadable Italian cheese, mascarpone is used in a number of dishes, both sweet and savory, and is a good substitute for clotted or Devonshire cream. Combined here with heavy cream, confectioners' sugar, and vanilla extract, it produces a decadent topping for cake.

¾ cup cold heavy whipping cream
¼ cup confectioners' sugar
½ teaspoon vanilla extract
½ cup mascarpone cheese

• In a medium bowl, beat together cream, sugar, and vanilla extract with a mixer at high speed until thick and creamy. Add mascarpone cheese, beating at medium-high speed until incorporated.

MAKE-AHEAD TIP: Frosting can be made a day in advance, placed in an airtight container, and refrigerated. Let come to room temperature and beat slightly before using.

Almond Tea Cookies

MAKES APPROXIMATELY 96

Petite round cookies rolled in pastel colored sugars and studded with blanched almonds are a wonderful offering for the final course of afternoon tea. This recipe makes enough cookies for guests to enjoy more than one or to take home as a parting gift.

1 cup unsalted butter, softened
¾ cup granulated sugar
1 large egg
1 teaspoon almond extract
⅛ teaspoon vanilla extract
2¼ cups all-purpose flour
1 teaspoon baking powder
¼ teaspoon fine sea salt
Various decorative colored sugars
Blanched almonds (1 per cookie)

• Preheat oven to 350°. Line several rimmed baking sheets with parchment paper.
• In a large mixing bowl, beat together butter and sugar with a mixer at medium speed until light and creamy, 2 to 3 minutes. Add egg, almond extract, and vanilla extract, beating until incorporated.
• In a medium bowl, whisk together flour, baking powder, and salt until combined. Add flour mixture to butter mixture, beating until incorporated.
• Place colored sugars in small, shallow bowls.
• Using a levered 1-teaspoon scoop, portion dough. Roll each dough ball between palms of hands to make a smooth ball. Roll each dough ball in colored sugar of choice and place 1 inch apart on prepared baking sheets. Press an almond into each dough ball.
• Bake until cookies are set with very light golden edges, 10 to 11 minutes. Transfer cookies to a wire cooling rack and let cool completely. Store in an airtight container with layers separated by wax paper.

MAKE-AHEAD TIP: Cookies can be made several weeks in advance, stored in an airtight container with layers separated by wax paper, and frozen.

Lemon Pavlovas

MAKES 12

This classic meringue dessert serves as a light, crisp nest to hold a fruit filling, like tangy lemon curd garnished with blueberries and fresh kiwi. While the meringue shells can be made up to a week in advance, they should be baked on a low-humidity day.

2 large egg whites, room temperature
¼ teaspoon cream of tartar
⅛ teaspoon fine sea salt
½ cup granulated sugar
¼ teaspoon vanilla extract
1 cup prepared lemon curd
½ cup blueberries
⅓ cup chopped kiwi
Garnish: melted apple jelly

• Preheat oven to 250°.
• Line a rimmed baking sheet with parchment paper. Using a 2-inch round cutter and a pencil, trace 12 circles, 2 inches apart, onto parchment paper, referring to page 130. Turn parchment paper over.
• In a large mixing bowl, beat together egg whites, cream of tartar, and salt with a mixer at high speed until soft peaks form. Add sugar and vanilla extract gradually, beating until stiff peaks form, approximately 5 minutes. (Meringue mixture will look glossy.)
• Transfer meringue mixture to a piping bag fitted with a medium open-star tip (Wilton #21).
• Referring to page 130 and starting in the middle of each traced circle, pipe concentric circles of meringue mixture outward until circle is filled. Pipe 1 to 2 extra layers on perimeters of rounds to form a rim around the edge of each circle.
• Bake for 1 hour. Turn oven off, open door, and let hot air escape. Close oven door and let meringue shells sit in oven for 2 hours or overnight. (This will help meringue shells continue to dry and become crisp.) Store meringue shells in an airtight container at room temperature until needed, up to a week.
• Just before serving, divide lemon curd among meringue shells. Top with blueberries and kiwi. Brush melted jelly on fruit to garnish, if desired. Serve immediately.

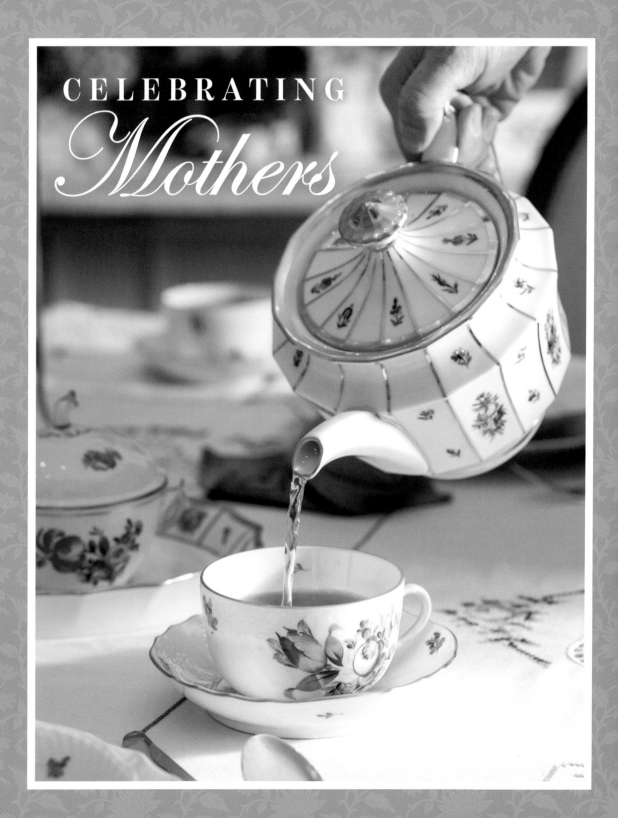

CELEBRATING
Mothers

The
MENU

SCONE
Sultana-Thyme Scones
First Flush Darjeeling Black Tea

SAVORIES
Balsamic-Pecan Chicken Salad
Tea Sandwiches
Cucumber-Tarragon Canapés
Tomato-Basil Quiche "Boxes"
*Organic Yunnan Golden Buds
Black Tea*

SWEETS
Raspberry-Orange Dacquoises
Jasmine-Honey Panna Cottas
Apricot Butter Cookies
Imperial Gold Oolong Tea

Tea Pairings by Mark T. Wendell Tea Company
978-635-9200 | marktwendell.com

*Surrounded by vibrant
florals, the special women
in your life will appreciate
a classic teatime held in
their honor.*

Sultana-Thyme Scones

MAKES 12

The sweetness from dried sultanas—a variety of grape that turns golden when dried—and the herbal notes of fresh thyme create a unique and refreshing scone that is sure to be a new favorite for afternoon tea.

2½ cups all-purpose flour
⅓ cup granulated sugar
1 tablespoon baking powder
½ teaspoon fine sea salt
4 tablespoons cold unsalted butter, cubed
½ cup sultanas or golden raisins
2 teaspoons chopped fresh thyme
½ cup plus 2 tablespoons cold heavy
    whipping cream, divided
1 large egg
½ teaspoon vanilla extract

• Preheat oven to 375°. Line a rimmed baking sheet with parchment paper.
• In a large bowl, whisk together flour, sugar, baking powder, and salt. Using a pastry blender or 2 forks, cut butter into flour mixture until it resembles coarse crumbs. Add sultanas and thyme, stirring until incorporated.
• In a small bowl, whisk together ½ cup plus 1 table-spoon cold cream, egg, and vanilla extract. Add to flour mixture, stirring until a dough begins to form. Working gently, bring mixture together with hands until a dough forms. (If mixture seems dry and a dough won't come together, add more cream, 1 tablespoon at a time.)
• Turn out dough onto a lightly floured surface, and knead gently by patting dough and folding it in half 5 to 7 times. Using a rolling pin, roll out dough to a 1-inch thickness. Using a 2¼-inch fluted round cutter dipped in flour, cut 12 scones from dough, rerolling scraps as needed. Place scones 2 inches apart on prepared baking sheet.
• Brush tops of scones with remaining 1 tablespoon cream.
• Bake until edges of scones are golden brown, 18 to 20 minutes.

RECOMMENDED CONDIMENTS:
Devonshire Cream
Lemon Curd
Orange Marmalade

Turn to page 127 for step-by-step instructions for the rosette napkin fold.

Balsamic-Pecan Chicken Salad Tea Sandwiches

MAKES 20

Golden balsamic vinegar and toasted pecans provide a welcome taste twist for the classic tea sandwich filling.

3 boneless, skinless chicken breasts
2 cups chicken broth
1 (6-inch) celery rib
1 green onion, coarsely chopped
3 sprigs fresh thyme
1 sprig fresh flat-leaf parsley
¾ cup mayonnaise
3 tablespoons golden balsamic vinegar
½ teaspoon fine sea salt
⅛ teaspoon ground black pepper
⅓ cup chopped toasted pecans
¼ cup finely chopped celery
10 slices firm honey wheat bread
Garnish: chopped fresh parsley

• In a large sauté pan, combine chicken breasts, chicken broth, celery rib, onion, thyme, and parsley. Bring to a slow simmer. Cover pan, and cook until chicken is white and opaque, 20 to 30 minutes. Let cool completely in pan. Transfer chicken to a cutting board. Using a sharp knife, coarsely chop chicken. Transfer chicken to the bowl of a food processor, and pulse until finely chopped.
• In a large bowl, whisk together mayonnaise, vinegar, salt, and pepper to combine. Add chicken, pecans, and chopped celery, stirring until well combined.
• Spread a thick, even layer of chicken salad onto 5 bread slices. Top each with a remaining bread slice to make 5 whole sandwiches.
• Using a serrated bread knife in a gentle sawing motion, trim and discard crusts from sandwiches, creating a perfect 3-inch square. Cut each sandwich diagonally into 4 equal triangles.
• Garnish cut sides with chopped parsley, if desired. Serve immediately.

MAKE-AHEAD TIP: Chicken salad can be made a day in advance, stored in a covered container, and refrigerated. Chicken salad sandwiches can be assembled up to 4 hours in advance, covered with damp paper towels, placed in an airtight container, and refrigerated. Garnish with parsley just before serving.

Cucumber-Tarragon Canapés

MAKES 18

Folded paper-thin slices of cucumber arranged together create a beautiful flower for an eye-catching canapé. Using a mandoline at the thinnest setting is key for making slices of identical thickness.

1 (8-ounce) package cream cheese, softened
1 tablespoon fresh lemon zest
2 teaspoons fresh lemon juice
2 teaspoons heavy whipping cream
¼ teaspoon fine sea salt
⅛ teaspoon ground black pepper
1 tablespoon chopped fresh tarragon
2 teaspoons chopped fresh flat-leaf parsley
1 English cucumber
18 round buttery crackers

• In a medium bowl, beat together cream cheese, lemon zest, lemon juice, cream, salt, and pepper with a mixer at medium-high speed until thick and creamy. Add tarragon and parsley, beating until combined.
• Using a mandoline or very sharp paring knife, cut cucumber into 90 paper-thin (¹⁄₁₆-inch) slices. Blot cucumber slices dry on paper towels.
• Place cream cheese mixture in a piping bag fitted with a large open-star tip (Wilton#1M). Pipe cream cheese mixture in an upright rosette onto crackers.
• Referring to page 129 for step-by-step photographs, fold each cucumber slice in half, and then in quarters. Pinch the inner fold of cucumber between thumb and forefinger. Place folded cucumber slice on canapé, green edges up, pressing lightly to adhere to cream cheese mixture. Repeat with 4 slices, placing last slice in center of canapé. Repeat with remaining cucumber slices and crackers. Serve immediately.

MAKE-AHEAD TIP: Cream cheese mixture can be made a day in advance, stored in an airtight container, and refrigerated. Let come to room temperature before using.

- Preheat oven to 350°. Spray a 9-inch square baking pan with baking spray with flour*.
- Using a colander, drain diced tomatoes. Blot dry on a paper towel.
- Scatter Fontina cheese, Parmesan cheese, tomatoes, and basil in even layers in prepared baking pan.
- In a large bowl, whisk together eggs, cream, salt, and pepper until well combined. Pour egg mixture over layers in pan.
- Bake until quiche is set and slightly puffed (it will still jiggle in pan slightly), 45 to 48 minutes. Let quiche cool completely in pan. Wrap pan with plastic wrap and refrigerate overnight.
- Using a sharp knife, trim and discard approximately ¼-inch of rough, browned edges. Cut remaining quiche into 16 equal squares. Using a small spatula, carefully transfer squares to a clean working surface.
- Using a sharp knife, cut prosciutto crosswise into ¼-inch-wide strips. Wrap quiche squares with prosciutto strips to look like a gift box, cutting and trimming excess as needed. Transfer quiche squares to a serving platter, and let come to room temperature.
- Garnish with fresh basil and yellow cherry tomato halves, if desired. Serve immediately.

If making this gluten-free, use cooking spray or olive oil to coat the baking pan instead.

Raspberry-Orange Dacquoises
MAKES 12

Dacquoises are iconic French pastries constructed of almond-meringue discs and filled with buttercream. Fresh raspberries not only add to the height of these treats (pictured on opposite page), but also to the flavor, especially when paired with Orange Buttercream. As with any meringue-based dessert, avoid making these on excessively humid days.

½ cup almond slices, toasted
3 large egg whites, room temperature
½ cup confectioners' sugar
¼ teaspoon cream of tartar
½ teaspoon vanilla extract
Orange Buttercream (recipe follows)
1 quart fresh raspberries

- Preheat oven to 250°. Trace 12 (2-inch) circles each onto 2 parchment paper sheets. Flip parchment paper over and place on 2 rimmed baking sheets.

Tomato-Basil Quiche "Boxes"
MAKES 16

For those not equipped with individual tartlet pans, preparing one quiche and cutting it into individual squares is a great alternative for serving this gluten-free savory. Dress up the individual portions with strips of prosciutto to mimic ribbons on a gift for a truly memorable presentation.

1 cup finely diced tomatoes
2 cups coarsely shredded Fontina cheese
½ cup freshly grated Parmesan cheese
2 tablespoons finely chopped fresh basil
6 large eggs
2 cups heavy whipping cream
½ teaspoon fine sea salt
¼ teaspoon ground black pepper
1 (4-ounce) package prosciutto slices
Garnish: fresh basil and yellow cherry tomato halves

- In the work bowl of a food processor, process almonds until finely ground, being careful not to make a nut butter.
- In the bowl of a stand mixer fitted with the paddle attachment, beat egg whites at high speed until foamy. Gradually add confectioners' sugar and cream of tartar, beating until stiff and glossy peaks form, approximately 6 minutes. Gently fold in almonds and vanilla extract until combined. Transfer meringue mixture to a piping bag fitted with a medium round tip (Wilton #12). Using drawn circles as guides, starting from the outer edges, pipe concentric circles of meringue mixture onto parchment paper until each drawn circle is filled.
- Bake until meringues are dry and crispy when touched, 50 to 60 minutes. Turn oven off and leave meringues in oven with door closed overnight to dry completely.
- Place Orange Buttercream in a piping bag fitted with an open-star tip (Wilton #1M), and pipe small rosettes around perimeter of 12 meringues. Place raspberries on buttercream around perimeter of meringues. Pipe a buttercream rosette into center hollow area of meringue, filling to height of raspberries (so when top meringues are placed, they will touch buttercream and will adhere). Cover each with a remaining meringue, flat side down. Pipe a buttercream rosette in center of meringues and top with a raspberry. Serve immediately, or store in an airtight container and refrigerate for up to 1 hour.

Orange Buttercream
MAKES 2 CUPS

An easy-to-assemble topping and filling for a number of desserts, buttercream is a favorite sweet spread, made even more delectable here with fresh orange zest.

1 cup unsalted butter, softened
4½ cups confectioners' sugar
3 tablespoons whole milk
1 tablespoon fresh orange zest
½ teaspoon vanilla extract
¼ teaspoon fine sea salt

- In a large bowl, beat together butter, sugar, milk, orange zest, vanilla extract, and salt with a mixer at high speed until light and fluffy. Use immediately.

Jasmine-Honey Panna Cottas
MAKES 6 (2-OUNCE) SERVINGS

Panna cotta is a traditional Italian dessert made of sweetened cream and set with unflavored gelatin. Infused with a jasmine tea and combined with orange blossom honey, this treat is delicious and especially stylish when served in petite coupe or martini glasses.

3 tablespoons water
1 (.25-ounce) envelope unflavored gelatin
2 cups heavy whipping cream
3 tablespoons loose jasmine tea leaves*
½ cup confectioners' sugar
1 tablespoon orange blossom honey
¼ teaspoon fine sea salt
¼ teaspoon vanilla extract
Garnish: chopped fresh strawberries
    and edible flowers**

• Place 3 tablespoons water in a small bowl. Sprinkle gelatin over water, and let stand for 10 minutes.
• In a medium saucepan, heat cream until an instant-read thermometer reads 190° to 200°. (Do not let cream come to a boil.) Remove saucepan from heat. Add tea leaves to heated cream, cover pan, and let steep for 5 minutes. Using a fine-mesh strainer, strain cream into a medium bowl, discarding tea leaves.
• Add gelatin mixture to steeped cream, whisking until combined. Add sugar, honey, salt, and vanilla extract, stirring until well combined. Transfer mixture to a liquid-measuring cup with a pouring spout. Let cool completely.
• Once cooled, pour panna cotta mixture into 6 (2-ounce) martini glasses, dividing evenly. Cover with plastic wrap, not letting plastic touch surface of panna cottas. Place on a rimmed baking sheet. Refrigerate panna cottas on baking sheet until set, approximately 4 hours.
• Garnish with edible flowers, if desired.

We used Yin Hao Jasmine Tea from Mark T. Wendell Tea Company, 978-635-9200, marktwendell.com.
**We used edible jasmine flowers from Gourmet Sweet Botanicals, 800-931-7530, gourmetsweetbotanicals.com.*

EDITOR'S NOTE: When steeping the tea in this recipe, it is important not to let the cream come to a boil. Steeping jasmine tea in boiling cream can cause the tea to become bitter.

Apricot Butter Cookies
MAKES 46

Using a piping bag fitted with a very large open-star tip to pipe the buttery dough for these cookies creates a pretty flower shape with a natural place for the fruit filling of choice. For a Mothers' Day tea party, apricot preserves is a delightful seasonal selection.

1 cup unsalted butter, softened
½ cup granulated sugar
½ teaspoon fine sea salt
1 large egg
½ teaspoon vanilla extract
¼ teaspoon almond extract
2¼ cups all-purpose flour
¾ cup apricot preserves

• Preheat oven to 400°. Line several rimmed baking sheets with parchment paper.
• In a large mixing bowl, beat together butter, sugar, and salt with a mixer at high speed until thick and creamy, approximately 4 minutes. Add egg, vanilla extract, and almond extract, beating until blended. Add flour, beating until combined.
• Transfer dough to a piping bag fitted with a very large open-star tip (Ateco #848). Pipe 1½-inch rosettes of dough 1 inch apart onto several baking sheets. Using the back of a floured ½-inch round measuring teaspoon or a floured thumb, make an indentation in the center of each cookie.
• Bake until cookies are set and edges are very light golden brown, 6 to 8 minutes. (Using a rounded measuring teaspoon, lightly press center indentations again, if necessary.) Transfer cookies to a wire cooling rack and let cool completely.
• Just before serving, place apricot preserves in a piping bag fitted with a medium round tip (Wilton#12), and pipe a button of preserves into centers of cookies.

KITCHEN TIP: If dough seems soft, chill dough for approximately 30 minutes to prevent spreading during baking. Dough does not need to be chilled if working in a cold kitchen.

CHERISHED
Thanksgiving

The
MENU

SCONE
Spiced Pumpkin Scones with
Sweetened Cream Cheese Spread

Cranberry Orange Tea

SAVORIES
Turkey & Cranberry
Puff Pastry Sandwiches

Apple Cider Vinegar Slaw
in Sweet Pepper Cups

Pecan-Fig Triple-Stack
Tea Sandwiches

Golden Monkey Black Tea

SWEETS
Sweet Potato Cakes with
Browned Butter Frosting

Walnut-Chocolate Blondie Bars

Apple Pie Tartlets with
Sweetened Whipped Cream

Honeybush Hazelnut

Tea Pairings by The Tea Shoppe
304-413-0890 | theteashoppewv.com

*Incorporate the flavors
of autumn into a teatime
menu full of recipes
inspired by favorite
Thanksgiving fare.*

Spiced Pumpkin Scones
MAKES 13 TO 16

While pumpkin is a popular filling for pie, it also adds flavor to scones, especially in combination with spices like cinnamon, ginger, allspice, mace, and cloves. Be sure to make the Sweetened Cream Cheese Spread to accompany these baked goods!

½ cup pumpkin purée
2½ cups all-purpose flour
⅓ cup firmly packed light brown sugar
1 tablespoon baking powder
1 teaspoon ground cinnamon
½ teaspoon ground ginger
½ teaspoon ground allspice
½ teaspoon fine sea salt
¼ teaspoon ground mace
⅛ teaspoon ground cloves
4 tablespoons cold unsalted butter, cubed
⅓ cup plus 2 tablespoons cold heavy cream, divided
1 large egg
½ teaspoon vanilla extract

• Preheat oven to 375°. Line a rimmed baking sheet with parchment paper.
• Line a small colander with paper towels. Place pumpkin in colander to drain of excess moisture.
• In a large bowl, whisk together flour, sugar, baking powder, cinnamon, ginger, allspice, salt, mace, and cloves until combined. Using a pastry blender or 2 forks, cut butter into flour mixture until it resembles coarse crumbs.
• In a small bowl, whisk together drained pumpkin, ⅓ cup cold cream, egg, and vanilla extract until combined. Add to flour mixture, stirring until a dough begins to form. Working gently, bring mixture together with hands until a dough forms. (If mixture seems dry and a dough won't come together, add more cream, 1 tablespoon at a time.)
• Turn out dough onto a lightly floured surface, and knead gently by patting dough and folding it in half 4 to 5 times. Using a rolling pin, roll out dough out to a 1-inch thickness. Using a 2-inch round cutter dipped in flour, cut as many scones as possible from dough, rerolling scraps as needed. Place scones 2 inches apart on prepared baking sheet.
• Brush tops of scones with remaining 1 tablespoon cream.
• Bake until edges of scones are golden brown and a wooden pick inserted in centers comes out clean, 18 to 20 minutes. Serve warm.

RECOMMENDED CONDIMENTS:
Sweetened Cream Cheese Spread (recipe follows)
Orange Marmalade

Sweetened Cream Cheese Spread
MAKES ½ CUP

Instead of traditional clotted or Devonshire cream, make your own spread for guests to slather on the Spiced Pumpkin Scones.

4 ounces cream cheese, softened
2 tablespoons confectioners' sugar
1 tablespoon heavy whipping cream

• In a small bowl, beat together cream cheese, sugar, and cream with a mixer at medium-high speed until combined.

MAKE-AHEAD TIP: Spread can be made up to 3 days in advance, covered, and refrigerated until needed. Let soften slightly at room temperature before using.

1 tablespoon water
¼ cup mayonnaise
2 teaspoons coarse-ground Dijon mustard
9 ultra-thin slices deli-style roast turkey
9 small leaves green leaf lettuce
Cranberry, Orange & Ginger Relish (recipe follows)

• Preheat oven to 400°. Line a rimmed baking sheet with parchment paper.
• Let puff pastry thaw slightly, but still remain firm. Using a sharp knife, cut 1 puff pastry sheet into 9 (2¾x2¼-inch) rectangles. Place puff pastry rectangles on prepared baking sheet.
• Using tip of a sharp knife or very small leaf-shaped cutters, cut 27 leaf shapes from remaining puff pastry sheet.
• In a small bowl, whisk together egg and 1 tablespoon water to make an egg wash. Brush egg wash over puff pastry rectangles. Arrange 3 leaves atop each rectangle. Brush leaves with egg wash.
• Bake until puff pastry is puffed and deep golden brown, 13 to 15 minutes.
• In a small bowl, stir together mayonnaise and mustard until combined.
• Using a sharp knife, carefully cut puff pastry rectangles in half horizontally. Spread mayonnaise mixture onto interior surfaces of puff pastry rectangles. On bottom halves of puff pastry rectangles, layer lettuce, a turkey slice (folding and ruffling to fit), and Cranberry, Orange & Ginger Relish. Cover with top halves of puff pastry rectangles. Serve immediately.

Cranberry, Orange & Ginger Relish
MAKES 1 CUP

A vibrant take on a Thanksgiving favorite, this cranberry relish, flavored with grated fresh ginger and orange zest, is perfect on a sandwich or on the side.

2 cups fresh cranberries
2 tablespoons granulated sugar
1 tablespoon fresh orange zest
½ teaspoon finely grated ginger

• In the work bowl of a food processor, pulse cranberries until very finely chopped.
• In a small bowl, stir together chopped cranberries, sugar, orange zest, and ginger until well combined. Store in a covered glass container and refrigerate until needed, up to a week.

Turkey & Cranberry Puff Pastry Sandwiches
MAKES 9

A Thanksgiving celebration just would not be complete without turkey and cranberries. This pretty sandwich variation, pictured on opposite page, incorporates both iconic flavors and uses puff pastry in lieu of sandwich bread. Although not mentioned in the recipe, traditional dressing or stuffing works well as an additional layer and is a great way to use leftovers.

1 (17.3-ounce) package frozen puff pastry (2 sheets)
1 large egg

Apple Cider Vinegar Slaw in Sweet Pepper Cups

MAKES 16

Petite sweet peppers are colorful, edible vessels for a made-from-scratch slaw that features the bright acidity of apple cider vinegar perfectly balanced with mayonnaise and a touch of sugar.

8 mini sweet peppers, mixed colors
¼ cup mayonnaise
2 teaspoons apple cider vinegar
1 teaspoon granulated sugar
¼ teaspoon fine sea salt
⅛ teaspoon ground black pepper
3 cups coarsely chopped cabbage
¼ cup coarsely chopped carrots

• Using a sharp knife, cut peppers in half horizontally. Using a spoon, scoop out and discard seeds and membranes. (Cut a small sliver from bottoms of pepper cups, if needed, to sit level.) Store pepper cups in a resealable plastic bag and refrigerate until needed, up to 2 days.
• In a medium bowl, whisk together mayonnaise, vinegar, sugar, salt, and black pepper until combined.
• In the work bowl of a food processor, pulse cabbage until very finely chopped. Transfer to a paper towel, and squeeze out any moisture. Clean out bowl of food processor. Repeat process with carrots.
• Add cabbage and carrots to mayonnaise mixture, stirring until combined. Cover slaw and refrigerate until chilled, up to 2 days.
• Just before serving, stir slaw well. Divide slaw among pepper cups.

Pecan-Fig Triple-Stack Tea Sandwiches

MAKES 9

Tangy goat cheese blends with smooth cream cheese, toasted pecans, and dried figs for the filling of this multi-stack sandwich.

4 ounces goat cheese, room temperature
4 ounces cream cheese, room temperature
2 teaspoons heavy whipping cream
1 teaspoon chopped fresh thyme
⅛ teaspoon fine sea salt
⅛ teaspoon ground black pepper
⅓ cup finely chopped dried figs
¼ cup finely chopped toasted pecans
9 slices very thin wheat bread, frozen
Garnish: fresh thyme sprigs

• In a medium bowl, beat together goat cheese, cream cheese, heavy cream, thyme, salt, and pepper with a mixer at medium-high speed until well combined. Add figs and pecans, beating until combined.
• Spread a thick, even layer of mixture onto 6 frozen bread slices. Stack bread slices in pairs, spread sides up, and top each with a plain bread slice to make 3 whole triple-stack sandwiches.
• Using a serrated bread knife in a gentle sawing motion, trim and discard crusts from sandwiches. Cut each sandwich into 3 rectangles. Cover with damp paper towels, and let thaw for several minutes before serving, or cover with damp paper towels, place in a covered container, and refrigerate for a few hours until ready to serve.
• Just before serving, garnish with fresh thyme sprigs, if desired.

Sweet Potato Cakes

MAKES 16

This moist cake featuring sweet potato and a number of seasonal spices is accompanied by a Browned Butter Frosting that lets the cake's complex combination of flavors shine. Stacking the delicate cake layers before cutting allows for a uniform presentation.

¾ cup unsalted butter, softened
½ cup granulated sugar
½ cup firmly packed light brown sugar
2 large eggs
1½ cups cake flour
1 teaspoon baking powder
¼ teaspoon baking soda
1 teaspoon ground cinnamon
¼ teaspoon ground mace
¼ teaspoon ground turmeric
¼ teaspoon fine sea salt
⅛ teaspoon ground black pepper
¾ cup sweet potato purée
¼ cup whole buttermilk
2 teaspoons vanilla extract
Browned Butter Frosting (recipe follows)
Garnish: orange zest curls

• Preheat oven to 350°. Spray a 13x9-inch baking pan with cooking spray. Line with parchment and spray again.
• In a large mixing bowl, beat together butter, granulated sugar, and brown sugar with a mixer at medium-high speed until light and fluffy, 3 to 5 minutes. Add eggs, one at a time, beating well after each addition until well incorporated.
• In a small bowl whisk together flour, baking powder, baking soda, cinnamon, mace, turmeric, salt, and pepper until combined.
• In another small bowl, stir together sweet potato purée, buttermilk, and vanilla extract until combined. Add flour mixture to butter mixture, alternately with sweet potato mixture, in thirds until well incorporated. Using an offset spatula, spread batter into prepared pan and smooth top to make surface level. Tap pan on countertop several times to level batter and reduce air bubbles.
• Bake until edges of cake are brown and a wooden pick inserted in center comes out clean, 16 to 18 minutes. Let cake cool completely in pan. Remove cake from pan and place on a cutting surface.

• Using a sharp knife, cut cake in half crosswise to create 2 (9x6½-inch) rectangles. Using an offset spatula, spread half of Browned Butter Frosting in an even layer on a cake half. Top with remaining cake half. Refrigerate cake for 10 minutes.
• Using a long, serrated bread knife in a gentle sawing motion and wiping knife between cuts, trim and discard edges from cake to create an 8x6-inch rectangle. Cut cake in half lengthwise, creating 2 (8x3-inch) rectangles. Cut each rectangle crosswise into 8 (3x1-inch) slices.
• Place remaining Browned Butter Frosting in a piping bag fitted with a small drop flower tip (Wilton #103). Pipe frosting decoratively onto tops of cake slices.
• Garnish with orange zest curls, if desired.

Browned Butter Frosting

MAKES 2¼ CUPS

Melting and cooking butter until it browns transforms its flavor, making it deeper, richer, and even slightly toasted and nutty. When cooled, browned butter can be used as the base for this fabulous frosting.

¾ cup salted butter, softened
2½ cups confectioners' sugar
2 teaspoons vanilla extract
¼ teaspoon fine sea salt
1 tablespoon whole milk
1 teaspoon heavy cream

• In a medium saucepan, melt butter over medium-high heat until it foams. Using a rubber spatula, scrape bottom of pan to keep butter from burning so it will brown evenly. (Lower heat, if necessary.) Let butter foam a second time. Stir, watching carefully so butter does not burn, until butter is a deep golden yellow and has a nutty aroma.
• Transfer browned butter to a heatproof bowl, and let come to room temperature. Refrigerate until butter becomes solid but soft enough to cream with a mixer.
• In a large mixing bowl, beat chilled browned butter with a mixer at medium speed until creamy, approximately 2 minutes. Add confectioners' sugar, beating at low speed until fluffy. Add vanilla extract and salt, beating to combine. Add milk and cream, beating at high speed until frosting is light and fluffy. Use immediately.

Walnut-Chocolate Blondie Bars

MAKES 24

Blondies laden with nuts and chocolate are simple sweets that can be made well in advance of afternoon tea.

1 cup unsalted butter, melted
2 cups firmly packed light brown sugar
2 large eggs
1 teaspoon vanilla extract
2 cups all-purpose flour
2 teaspoons baking powder
½ teaspoon fine sea salt
1⅓ cups chopped toasted walnuts, divided
1 cup dark chocolate chips
½ cup semisweet chocolate chips
1 tablespoon turbinado sugar

• Preheat oven to 350°. Spray a 13x9-inch baking pan with cooking spray. Line pan with parchment paper and spray again.
• In a large bowl, beat together butter and brown sugar with a mixer at low speed until well combined. Add eggs and vanilla extract, beating until incorporated.
• In a medium bowl, whisk together flour, baking powder, and salt until combined. Add flour mixture to egg mixture, beating until combined. Add 1 cup walnuts, dark chocolate chips, and semisweet chocolate chips, stirring until combined.
• Using an offset spatula, spread batter into prepared pan, smoothing top. Sprinkle with remaining ⅓ cup walnuts and turbinado sugar.
• Bake until edges are golden brown and a wooden pick inserted in center comes out clean, 25 to 30 minutes. Let cool completely in pan on a wire cooling rack.
• Remove from pan and place on a cutting surface. Using a long, sharp knife, trim and discard rough edges. Cut into 24 bars. Wrap bars in plastic wrap and place in an airtight container until ready to serve, up to 2 days.

MAKE-AHEAD TIP: Bars can be made up to a week in advance, wrapped in plastic wrap, placed in an airtight container, and frozen. Let come to room temperature before serving. To soften chocolate chips, warm bars slightly in a 300° oven for approximately 5 minutes, if desired.

Apple Pie Tartlets

MAKES 24

Tea-size miniature tartlets that fit easily on a tiered stand allow guests to enjoy the classic Thanksgiving dessert at afternoon tea.

3 cups all-purpose flour
¾ teaspoon fine sea salt
1 cup cold unsalted butter, cubed
⅓ cup ice water
1 tablespoon white distilled vinegar
1 large egg
Apple Pie Filling (recipe follows)
Sweetened Whipped Cream (recipe follows)
Garnish: apple slice slivers

• In a large bowl, whisk together flour and salt until combined. Using a pastry blender or 2 forks, cut in butter until it resembles coarse crumbs.
• In a small bowl, whisk together ⅓ cup ice water, vinegar, and egg until combined. Add to flour mixture, stirring with a fork until evenly moist. Working gently with hands, bring mixture together until a dough forms. Divide dough into 4 equal portions, and wrap each portion with plastic wrap. Refrigerate dough portions until very firm, but still pliable to work with, 1 to 2 hours.
• Preheat oven to 425°. Lightly spray 24 (2¼-inch) fluted tartlet pans with cooking spray.
• Working with one dough portion at a time, turn out dough onto a lightly floured surface. Using a rolling pin, roll out dough to a ⅛-inch thickness. Using a 2¾-inch round cutter dipped in flour, cut 6 rounds from dough. Being careful not to stretch dough, center a dough round atop each prepared tartlet pan. Lightly press dough rounds into bottom of tartlet pans, and stand dough up against sides of pans. Using a rolling pin, roll over top of tartlet pans to trim excess dough. Using wide end of a chopstick and referring to page 129, press dough into indentations in sides of tartlet pans. Lightly prick bottoms with a fork. Place a small piece of parchment paper in center of each prepared tartlet pan, letting ends extend over edges of pan, and place ceramic pie weights or dried beans atop each parchment piece.
• Bake until light golden brown, 5 to 7 minutes. Let cool on a wire rack. Remove pie weights and parchment paper.
• Bake tartlet shells again until lightly browned, approximately 3 minutes. Let cool completely in pans. Remove tartlet shells from pans and store in an airtight container until needed, up to a day.
• Just before serving, divide Apple Pie Filling among tartlet shells. Top each with a dollop of Sweetened Whipped Cream.
• Garnish with an apple slice sliver, if desired.

Apple Pie Filling

MAKES 2 CUPS

Apples cooked in a myriad of spices make for a flavorful filling for individual tartlets.

2 tablespoons unsalted butter
4 cups very small diced peeled apples*
¼ cup granulated sugar
½ teaspoon ground cinnamon
¼ teaspoon ground mace
¼ teaspoon ground allspice
⅛ teaspoon fine sea salt
1 teaspoon fresh lemon juice
1 tablespoon water

• In a large sauté pan, heat butter over medium-high heat until it melts. Add apples, sugar, cinnamon, mace, allspice, salt, lemon juice, and 1 tablespoom water, stirring to combine. Cook until mixture is well combined, and then turn heat to low and cover pan. Cook, stirring occasionally, until apples are very tender and mixture has thickened slightly, approximately 10 to 15 minutes. If mixture starts to dry out, add more water, 1 teaspoon at a time. Let cool before using.

We used 1 Granny Smith apple, 1 Gala apple, and 1 Golden Delicious apple.

MAKE-AHEAD TIP: Filling can be made a day in advance and stored in a covered container in the refrigerator. Rewarm gently in a sauté pan before using.

Sweetened Whipped Cream

MAKES 2 CUPS

A dollop of this topping adds extra sweetness to a number of desserts, including our Apple Pie Tartlets.

¾ cup cold heavy whipping cream
2 tablespoons confectioners' sugar
¼ teaspoon vanilla extract

• In a deep bowl, beat together cold cream, confectioners' sugar, and vanilla extract with a mixer at high speed until thick and creamy. Use immediately.

EVERGREEN
Christmas

The
MENU

SCONE
Panettone Scones
Gingerbread Black Tea

SAVORIES
Beet & Cucumber Canapés
Roast Beef & Bacon Tea Sandwiches
Salmon & Chive Crostini with
Sweet Chili Glaze
*Organic Tippy Colombian
Black Tea (T2)*

SWEETS
Cherry-Coconut Divinity
Pistachio-Chocolate Shortbreads
Citrus Cakes
Roasted Chestnut Rooibos

Tea Pairings by Simpson & Vail
800-282-8327 | svtea.com

*Spread holiday cheer by
inviting guests to gather
around a beautifully
adorned table for an
unforgettable teatime.*

Panettone Scones

MAKES 16

Panettone is a fruitcake-like bread hailing from the city of Milan. As the sweet Italian bread is traditionally prepared as part of Yuletide (and even New Year's) festivities, this scone is a wonderful variation on the classic treat. If you don't want to soak the dried fruits in liqueur, you may substitute orange juice.

¼ cup dried cranberries
¼ cup dried currants
¼ cup golden raisins
1 cup orange liqueur*
2½ cups all-purpose flour
¼ cup plus 1 tablespoon granulated sugar, divided
1 tablespoon baking powder
½ teaspoon fine sea salt
¼ cup cold unsalted butter, cubed
½ cup plus 1 tablespoon cold heavy whipping cream, divided
2 large eggs, divided
½ teaspoon vanilla extract

Turn to page 128 for step-by-step instructions for the Christmas tree napkin fold.

• In a small bowl, combine cranberries, currants, and raisins. Pour orange liqueur over dried fruits until covered. Cover bowl with plastic wrap, and let sit at room temperature overnight to soak.
• Preheat oven to 375°. Line a rimmed baking sheet with parchment paper.
• Drain soaked fruits completely.
• In a large bowl, whisk together flour, ¼ cup sugar, baking powder, and salt. Using a pastry blender or 2 forks, cut butter into flour mixture until it resembles coarse crumbs. Stir in drained fruit.
• In a small bowl, whisk together ½ cup cream, 1 egg, and vanilla extract until well combined. Add to flour mixture, stirring until a dough begins to form. Working gently, bring mixture together with hands until a dough forms. (If mixture seems dry and dough won't come together, add more cream, 1 tablespoon at a time.)
• Turn out dough onto a lightly floured surface, and knead gently until smooth by patting dough and folding it in half 8 to 10 times. Using a rolling pin, roll out dough to a ¾-inch thickness. Using a 2-inch round cutter dipped in flour, cut 16 scones from dough, rerolling scraps as needed. Place scones 2 inches apart on prepared baking sheet.
• In a small bowl, whisk together remaining egg and 1 tablespoon cream. Brush lightly over tops of scones. Sprinkle with remaining 1 tablespoon sugar.

• Bake until scones are golden brown and a wooden pick inserted in centers comes out clean, 17 to 19 minutes. Serve warm.

RECOMMENDED CONDIMENTS:
Devonshire Cream
Red Currant Jam
Orange Marmalade

*Triple Sec or Grand Marnier can be used.

KITCHEN TIP: For a neat appearance, use kitchen scissors to trim pertruding fruits from sides of scones before baking.

Beet & Cucumber Canapés

MAKES 12

Incorporating cooked, chopped beet in an herbaceous cream cheese mixture creates a beautiful hue. Pipe this topping over an additional filling of beets and green cucumber for canapés that are as visually vibrant as they are appetizing.

1 small red beet
⅛ teaspoon olive oil
¼ teaspoon fine sea salt, divided
1 (8-ounce) package cream cheese, softened
1 tablespoon finely chopped fresh dill
⅜ teaspoon granulated shallot
⅛ teaspoon ground black pepper
1 tablespoon heavy whipping cream
1 English cucumber
Garnish: fresh dill sprigs

• Preheat oven to 350°.
• Wash beet well and dry completely. Place beet on a square of foil. Drizzle with olive oil and sprinkle with ⅛ teaspoon salt. Pull edges of foil together to encase beet, sealing foil. Place on a rimmed baking sheet.
• Bake for 1 hour. Let beet cool completely before peeling. (Wear latex gloves to prevent beet from staining fingers, if desired.)
• Place peeled beet in the work bowl of a food processor, and pulse to finely chop. Drain chopped beet, if necessary.
• In a medium bowl, beat together cream cheese, dill, shallot, remaining ⅛ teaspoon salt, pepper, and heavy cream with a mixer at medium-high speed until combined and creamy. Add 2 tablespoons chopped beet, stirring until well blended.
• Using a Y-shaped vegetable peeler, peel lengthwise strips from cucumber, creating a striped effect. Using a sharp knife, cut 12 (½-inch) slices. Using a mini melon baller tool, scoop centers out of each slice to make cups. Blot cucumber cups dry on paper towels.
• Transfer cream cheese mixture to a piping bag fitted with a large open-star tip (Wilton #1M).
• Blot remaining chopped beet on paper towels. Divide beet among cucumber cups. Pipe an upright dollop of cream cheese mixture on top of beet.
• Garnish each with a fresh dill sprig, if desired. Serve immediately.

MAKE-AHEAD TIP: Beet can be prepared a day in advance, stored in a covered container, and refrigerated. Cucumber cups can be made a day in advance, wrapped in a damp paper towel, stored in a resealable plastic bag, and refrigerated. Cream cheese mixture can be made a day in advance, stored in an airtight container, and refrigerated. (Color will deepen overnight.) Let cream cheese mixture come to room temperature before using.

Roast Beef & Bacon Tea Sandwiches

MAKES 9

When it comes to tea sandwiches, more filling is better. Layers of mustard aïoli, arugula, roast beef, bacon, and tomato create a hearty and flavorful option for the savory course of afternoon tea.

2 tablespoons coarse-ground Dijon mustard
2 tablespoons mayonnaise
6 large slices firm white sandwich bread
3 cups loosely packed arugula
12 ultra-thin slices roast beef
6 thin slices bacon, cooked
12 slices Campari tomato
½ teaspoon extra-virgin olive oil
½ teaspoon red wine vinegar
⅛ teaspoon fresh ground black pepper

• In a small bowl, stir together mustard and mayonnaise to make an aïoli. Spread an even layer of aïoli onto bread slices.
• Place a layer of arugula over aïoli on a bread slice. Place 4 roast beef slices, folded and ruffled to fit bread slice, over arugula. Cover beef with 2 bacon slices. Place 4 tomato slices over bacon. Cover bacon with another layer of arugula. Drizzle arugula lightly with olive oil and red wine vinegar. Sprinkle with fresh ground pepper. Top with another bread slice, aïoli side down. Repeat with remaining ingredients to make 3 whole sandwiches.
• Using a serrated bread knife in a gentle sawing motion, trim and discard crusts from sandwiches. Cut each sandwich into 3 (3x1¼-inch) rectangles. Serve immediately, or cover with a damp paper towels, place in a covered container, and refrigerate for a few hours until ready to serve.

- Fold salmon slices to fit bread slices (crostini).
- In a small bowl, stir together sweet chili sauce and soy sauce until combined.
- Just before serving, place a folded salmon slice on each crostini. Brush salmon slices with sauce mixture.
- Garnish each crostini with a chive bud, if desired. Serve immediately.

Cherry-Coconut Divinity
MAKES APPROXIMATELY 48

This light, chewy candy, pictured on opposite page, is a popular Southern sweet that has a consistency similar to nougat. So it will set properly, this confection is best prepared on days with little to no humidity.

2½ cups granulated sugar
½ cup light corn syrup
½ cup water
¼ teaspoon fine sea salt
2 large egg whites, room temperature
1 teaspoon coconut extract
½ cup chopped candied cherries
¼ cup unsweetened coconut flakes

- Line 2 rimmed baking sheets with wax paper. Lightly spray with cooking spray. Lightly spray 2 teaspoons with cooking spray.
- In a large saucepan, combine sugar, corn syrup, ½ cup water, and salt. Cook over medium-high heat, stirring just until sugar dissolves and temperature reaches 260° on an instant-read or candy thermometer. (Mixture will thicken slightly as it reaches 260°.)
- As mixture is cooking, place egg whites in the bowl of a stand mixer. Beat egg whites at high speed until stiff peaks form. With mixer on, add hot sugar syrup to beaten egg whites in a thin, steady stream, beating until incorporated. Add coconut extract, beating until mixture holds its shape and begins to lose its glossy appearance, approximately 5 minutes. Add cherries and coconut flakes, stirring until well incorporated.
- Using prepared spoons and working quickly, immediately drop mixture by rounded teaspoonfuls onto prepared baking sheets. Let stand until firm and dry to touch before removing from baking sheets, approximately 6 hours. Place in bonbon cups, if desired. Store in an airtight container at room temperature with layers separated by wax paper.

Salmon & Chive Crostini with Sweet Chili Glaze
MAKES 12

A sweet chili glaze softens the briny taste of smoked salmon in this savory canapé. Serve this flavorful combination on slices of French bread that have been spread with an herb-lime butter and perfectly toasted.

4 tablespoons salted butter, room temperature
1 tablespoon chopped flat-leaf parsley
½ teaspoon chopped fresh chives
½ teaspoon fresh lime zest
½ teaspoon fresh lime juice
12 (½-inch) slices French bread
12 slices smoked salmon
2 tablespoons Asian sweet chili sauce
½ teaspoon low-sodium soy sauce
Garnish: fresh chive buds

- Preheat oven to 350°.
- In a small bowl, stir together butter, parsley, chives, lime zest, and lime juice until combined. Spread an even layer of butter mixture onto French bread slices. Place bread slices, butter side up, on a rimmed baking sheet.
- Bake until bread is toasted, approximately 7 minutes. Let cool. Store in an airtight container until needed.

Pistachio-Chocolate Shortbreads

MAKES APPROXIMATELY 36

Dutch-process cocoa gives these cookies a marvelous, sweet taste. Roll the dough portions in granulated sugar and sprinkle with salted pistachios just before baking, and dip the bottoms of the cooled cookies in melted dark chocolate for a decadent teatime treat.

2 cups all-purpose flour
⅓ cup plus 2 tablespoons Dutch-process cocoa
    powder
⅓ cup confectioners' sugar
½ cup granulated sugar, divided
2 tablespoons firmly packed light brown sugar
¼ teaspoon fine sea salt
1 cup plus 2 tablespoons unsalted butter, room
    temperature
½ teaspoon vanilla extract
⅓ cup finely chopped roasted, salted pistachios
1 (10-ounce) package dark chocolate–flavored melting
    wafers*

• Preheat oven to 325°. Line 2 rimmed baking sheets with parchment paper.
• In a large bowl, whisk together flour, cocoa powder, confectioners' sugar, ¼ cup granulated sugar, brown sugar, and salt until combined. (If cocoa powder or confectioners' sugar is lumpy, sift mixture through a sieve.)
• Using a pastry blender or 2 forks, cut butter into flour mixture until it resembles coarse crumbs. Add vanilla extract, stirring until combined. Gather mixture together with hands to form a dough.
• Using a levered 1-tablespoon scoop, portion dough and place approximately 1-inch apart on prepared baking sheets.
• Place remaining ¼ cup granulated sugar in a small bowl. Lightly dip tops of cookie dough balls in sugar, and return to baking sheets. Using the bottom of a drinking glass, press down lightly on sugared tops of cookies. Sprinkle tops of cookies with chopped pistachios. Using the bottom of drinking glass, press down lightly so pistachios adhere to cookies.
• Bake until cookies are set, approximately 15 minutes, rotating baking pans halfway through for even baking. Let cookies rest on baking sheet for approximately 1 minute before transferring cookies to a wire cooling rack. Let cool completely.

• Melt chocolate melting wafers according to package directions. Dip bottoms of cooled cookies into melted chocolate, and place chocolate side up onto cooling racks. Let chocolate set. Store cookies for up to 1 week at room temperature in an airtight container with layers separated by wax paper.

*We used Ghirardelli.

Citrus Cakes

MAKES APPROXIMATELY 15 SERVINGS

Instead of slicing a two-layer cake, cut it into squares that will work perfectly on any tiered stand. Guests will find the small, even portions brimming with the flavors of lemon and orange.

½ cup plus 2 tablespoons unsalted butter,
    room temperature
1½ cups granulated sugar
1 tablespoon fresh orange zest
2 teaspoons fresh lemon zest
3 large eggs, room temperature
2½ cups cake flour*
2½ teaspoons baking powder
¾ teaspoon fine sea salt
¾ cup whole milk
2 tablespoons fresh lemon juice
Citrus Butter Frosting (recipe follows)
Garnish: fresh rosemary sprigs and fresh orange
    zest strips

• Preheat oven to 375°. Spray a 17¼x11½x1-inch rimmed baking sheet with baking spray with flour. Line with parchment paper. Spray parchment paper.
• In a large bowl, beat together butter, sugar, and zests with a mixer at high speed until light and fluffy, approximately 3 minutes. Add eggs, one at a time, beating well after each addition.
• In a medium bowl, whisk together flour, baking powder, and salt. Add flour mixture alternately with milk and lemon juice, beginning and ending with flour mixture, beating well after each addition.
• Spread batter into prepared pan. Using an offset spatula, smooth top to make level. Tap pan on countertop a few times to level batter and reduce air bubbles.
• Bake until edges are golden brown and a wooden pick inserted in center comes out clean, 12 to 14 minutes. Let cake cool completely in pan.
• Turn out cake onto a cutting surface. Using a serrated bread knife in a gentle sawing motion, cut cake in half crosswise.

• Using an offset spatula, spread half of Citrus Butter Frosting in an even layer onto one cake half. Top with remaining cake half. Using an offset spatula, spread remaining half of frosting in an even layer onto top of cake. To make cake easier to cut, freeze cake on cutting board for approximately 30 minutes.
• Using a long sharp knife and pressing knife in a downward motion, trim and discard an approximately 1-inch border on all sides of cake. Cut cake into 1½-inch squares.
• Garnish with fresh rosemary and orange zest strips, if desired. Serve immediately.

*To measure flour accurately, whisk flour well. Spoon flour into a measuring cup, and level off without packing.

MAKE-AHEAD TIP: Cake can be baked earlier in the day, assembled, cut into squares, placed in an airtight container, and refrigerated. Let cake squares come to room temperature before garnishing and serving.

IMPORTANT KITCHEN TIP: Do not combine milk and lemon juice before incorporating into cake batter or milk will curdle. Add to butter mixture separately and alternately with flour mixture.

Citrus Butter Frosting

MAKES APPROXIMATELY 3 CUPS

In this buttercream, the combination of sweet orange and sour lemon zests and juices are so good, one layer won't be enough.

5¼ cups confectioners' sugar
½ cup unsalted butter, room temperature
¼ teaspoon fine sea salt
2 teaspoons fresh orange zest
2 teaspoons fresh lemon zest
¼ cup fresh orange juice
1 tablespoon fresh lemon juice

• In a large bowl, beat together sugar, butter, salt, zests, and juices with a mixer at low speed until combined, scraping down sides bowl as necessary. Increase speed to high and beat until light and fluffy. Use immediately.

Scones

Cinnamon-Currant Scones

MAKES 12

Dried currant, a variety of grape, is a classic addition
to English scones, as its small size packs a flavorful punch.

3 cups all-purpose flour
⅓ cup granulated sugar
4 teaspoons baking powder
1½ teaspoons ground cinnamon
½ teaspoon fine sea salt
8 tablespoons cold unsalted butter, cubed
½ cup dried currants
1 cup plus 1 tablespoon cold heavy whipping cream,
   divided
1 large egg
Garnish: sparkling sugar

• Preheat oven to 400°. Line a rimmed baking sheet
with parchment paper.
• In a large bowl, whisk together flour, granulated sugar,
baking powder, cinnamon, and salt. Using a pastry
blender or 2 forks, cut in cold butter until it resembles
coarse crumbs. Stir in currants. Add 1 cup cold cream,
stirring with a fork just until dry ingredients are moistened. Working gently, bring mixture together with hands
until a dough forms. (If dough seems dry and won't come
together, add more cream, 1 tablespoon at a time.)
• Turn out dough onto a lightly floured surface, and
knead gently until smooth by patting dough and folding it in half 4 to 5 times. Cover and let rest at room
temperature for 15 minutes. Using a rolling pin, roll out
dough to a ¾-inch thickness. Using a 2¼-inch fluted
round cutter dipped in flour, cut 12 scones from dough,
rerolling scraps as necessary. Place scones 2 inches
apart on prepared baking sheet.
• In a small bowl, whisk together egg and remaining
1 tablespoon cold cream. Brush tops of scones with egg
mixture. Garnish tops with sparkling sugar, if desired.
• Bake until tops of scones are golden and a wooden pick
inserted in centers comes out clean, 12 to 15 minutes.
Serve warm.

RECOMMENDED CONDIMENTS:
Devonshire Cream
Seedless Blackberry Jam

Zucchini-Walnut Scones
MAKES 18

A bit of a play on zucchini bread, these surprisingly sweet scones are made with whole-wheat flour and are studded with toasted walnuts and dried currants. They are especially delightful when accompanied by Creamy Brown Sugar Spread.

2½ cups whole-wheat flour
1 cup all-purpose flour
⅓ cup firmly packed light brown sugar
1 tablespoon baking powder
½ teaspoon fine sea salt
½ teaspoon ground allspice
¼ teaspoon ground nutmeg
6 tablespoons cold unsalted butter, cubed
1 cup coarsely grated zucchini, squeezed dry
⅓ cup chopped toasted walnuts
⅓ cup dried currants
¾ cup cold heavy whipping cream
¼ cup cold whole milk
½ teaspoon vanilla extract

• Preheat oven to 350°. Line a rimmed baking sheet with parchment paper.
• In a large bowl, whisk together both flours, brown sugar, baking powder, salt, allspice, and nutmeg. Using a pastry blender or 2 forks, cut butter into flour mixture until it resembles coarse crumbs. Add zucchini, walnuts, and currants, stirring well.
• In a small bowl, combine cream, milk, and vanilla extract, stirring to blend. Add to flour mixture, stirring until mixture comes together. Working gently, bring mixture together with hands until a dough forms. (If dough seems dry and won't come together, add more cream, 1 tablespoon at a time.)
• Turn out dough onto a lightly floured surface, and knead gently until smooth by patting dough and folding it in half 4 to 5 times. Using a rolling pin, roll out dough to a ¾-inch thickness. Using a 2-inch fluted square cutter dipped in flour, cut 18 scones from dough. Place scones 2 inches apart on prepared baking sheet.
• Bake until edges of scones are golden brown and a wooden pick inserted in centers comes out clean, approximately 20 minutes.

RECOMMENDED CONDIMENT:
Creamy Brown Sugar Spread (recipe follows)

Creamy Brown Sugar Spread
MAKES ½ CUP

Cream cheese and salted butter are the base for this flavorful spread that is sweetened with light brown sugar.

4 ounces cream cheese, softened
4 tablespoons salted butter, softened
¼ cup firmly packed light brown sugar
¼ teaspoon vanilla extract

• In a small mixing bowl, beat together cream cheese, butter, brown sugar, and vanilla extract with a mixer at medium speed until light and creamy. Use immediately, or cover and refrigerate until needed, up to a week.

EDITOR'S NOTE: For an attractive presentation, place Creamy Brown Sugar Spread in a piping bag fitted with a large open-star tip (Wilton #1M) and pipe individual servings into antique salt cellars or other small bowls.

- In a large bowl, mash squash pulp with a fork until smooth. Cover and refrigerate until chilled, approximately 30 minutes.
- Line another rimmed baking sheet with parchment paper.
- In the work bowl of a food processor, pulse together flour, granulated sugar, baking powder, sage, salt, and cinnamon until combined. Add cold butter, pulsing until it resembles coarse crumbs. Transfer mixture to a large bowl. Add squash and ¼ cup cream, stirring until a dough forms.
- Turn out dough onto a lightly floured surface, and knead gently until smooth by patting dough and folding it in half 5 to 7 times. Using a rolling pin, roll out dough to a ¾-inch thickness. Using a 2-inch fluted round cutter dipped in flour, cut 16 scones from dough, rerolling scraps as necessary. Place scones 2 inches apart on prepared baking sheet. Freeze for 10 minutes.
- In a small bowl, whisk together egg and remaining 1 tablespoon cream. Brush tops of scones with egg mixture, and sprinkle with cane sugar.
- Bake until edges of scones are golden brown and a wooden pick inserted in centers comes out clean, 15 to 18 minutes. Serve warm.

RECOMMENDED CONDIMENT:
Devonshire Cream

Butternut Squash Scones
MAKES 16

Roasted butternut squash and chopped fresh sage combine to add seasonally appropriate flavors to these Thanksgiving-inspired scones.

1 small (approximately 1-pound) butternut squash
2 cups all-purpose flour
¼ cup plus 2 tablespoons granulated sugar
1 tablespoon baking powder
1 tablespoon chopped fresh sage
½ teaspoon fine sea salt
½ teaspoon ground cinnamon
8 tablespoons cold unsalted butter, cubed
¼ cup plus 1 tablespoon cold heavy whipping cream, divided
1 large egg
2 tablespoons cane sugar

- Preheat oven to 400°. Line a rimmed baking sheet with foil.
- Using a sharp knife, cut squash in half lengthwise. Using a spoon, scoop out and discard seeds. Place squash halves, cut sides down, on prepared baking sheet. Pierce top side of squash several times with a fork.
- Bake until squash is tender, 35 to 40 minutes. Let cool for 10 minutes. Peel and discard skin from squash.

Mango-Lime Gluten-free Scones
MAKES 8

The tropical notes of lime and mango will undoubtedly make this a new favorite. If using fresh mango, make sure to select one that smells very sweet. You can also find ripe mango in jars in the canned fruit section of most grocery stores.

2 cups gluten-free all-purpose flour blend*
⅓ cup plus 1 tablespoon granulated sugar, divided
2 teaspoons baking powder
1 teaspoon fresh lime zest
½ teaspoon fine sea salt
4 tablespoons cold unsalted butter, cubed
¾ cup plus 3 tablespoons cold heavy whipping cream, divided
½ teaspoon vanilla extract
½ cup diced ripe mango, divided

- Preheat oven to 350°. Line a rimmed baking sheet with parchment paper.

• In a large bowl, whisk together flour, ⅓ cup sugar, baking powder, lime zest, and salt. Using a pastry blender or 2 forks, cut butter into flour mixture until it resembles coarse crumbs.

• In a liquid-measuring cup, combine ¾ cup plus 2 tablespoons cream and vanilla extract, stirring well. Add to flour mixture stirring until mixture is evenly moist. Working gently, bring mixture together with hands until a dough forms. (If dough seems dry and won't come together, add more cream, 1 tablespoon at a time.)

• Turn out dough onto a lightly floured* surface, and knead gently until smooth by patting dough and folding it in half 4 to 5 times. Using a rolling pin, roll out dough to a ½-inch thickness. Scatter ¼ cup mango over half of dough. Fold other half of dough over mango to enclose it. Gently roll out dough to a ½-inch thickness again. Repeat scattering and folding with remaining ¼ cup mango. Gently roll out dough to a 1-inch thickness.

Using a 2¼-inch round cutter dipped in flour*, cut 8 scones from dough, rerolling scraps as needed. Place scones 2 inches apart on prepared baking sheet.

• Brush tops of scones with remaining 1 tablespoon cream. Sprinkle tops of scones with remaining 1 table-spoon sugar.

• Bake until edges are golden brown and a wooden pick inserted in centers comes out clean, 18 to 20 minutes. Serve warm.

*We used Pamela's Gluten-Free All-Purpose Flour Artisan Blend. King Arthur's Gluten-Free Measure for Measure Flour or Bob's Red Mill Gluten Free 1-to-1 Baking Flour can also be used. For tips on using conventional flour (with gluten), turn to page 96.

RECOMMENDED CONDIMENT:
Key Lime Curd (recipe on page 28)

Nutmeg–Dried Tangerine Scones

MAKES 12

A tangy buttermilk dough is the base of these inventive scones that are laced with ground nutmeg and bits of dried tangerine. To add a festive touch to the platter, garnish with curls of tangerine peel.

2½ cups all-purpose flour
¼ cup firmly packed light brown sugar
1½ teaspoons baking powder
¼ teaspoon fine sea salt
¼ teaspoon baking soda
½ teaspoon ground nutmeg, divided
¼ cup plus 1 tablespoon cold unsalted butter, cubed
½ cup finely chopped dried tangerine
¾ cup plus 1 tablespoon cold whole buttermilk, divided
1 large egg

• Preheat oven to 375°. Line a rimmed baking sheet with parchment paper.
• In a large bowl, whisk together flour, brown sugar, baking powder, salt, baking soda, and ¼ teaspoon nutmeg. Using a pastry blender or 2 forks, cut in cold butter until it resembles coarse crumbs. Add tangerine, stirring until combined. Add ¾ cup cold buttermilk, stirring with a fork just until dry ingredients are moistened. Working gently, bring mixture together with hands until a dough forms. (If dough seems dry and won't come together, add more buttermilk, 1 tablespoon at a time.)
• Turn out dough onto a lightly floured surface, and knead gently until smooth by patting dough and folding it in half 4 to 5 times. Using a rolling pin, roll out dough to a ¾-inch thickness. Using a 2-inch fluted round cutter dipped in flour, cut 12 scones from dough, rerolling scraps as necessary. Place scones 2 inches apart on prepared baking sheet. Freeze for 10 minutes.
• In a small bowl, whisk together egg, remaining 1 tablespoon cold buttermilk, and remaining ¼ teaspoon nutmeg. Brush egg mixture onto tops of scones.
• Bake until scones are golden brown and a wooden pick inserted in centers comes out clean, 15 to 18 minutes. Serve warm.

RECOMMENDED CONDIMENTS:
Devonshire Cream
Orange Marmalade

Spiced Cream Cheese Scones
MAKES 18

A quintet of spices flavor these decadent baked goods made primarily with bread flour but with a small amount of cake flour added for the best texture.

2 cups bread flour
¼ cup cake flour
½ cup granulated sugar
2½ teaspoons baking powder
½ teaspoon kosher salt
½ teaspoon ground cinnamon, divided
½ teaspoon ground cloves, divided
½ teaspoon ground allspice, divided
½ teaspoon ground nutmeg, divided
½ teaspoon ground ginger, divided
4 tablespoons cold unsalted butter, cubed
4 ounces cold cream cheese, cubed
1 cup plus 2 tablespoons cold heavy whipping cream, divided

• Preheat oven to 400°. Line 2 rimmed baking sheets with parchment paper.
• In a medium bowl, whisk together both flours, sugar, baking powder, salt, ¼ teaspoon cinnamon, ¼ teaspoon cloves, ¼ teaspoon allspice, ¼ teaspoon nutmeg, and ¼ teaspoon ginger. Using a pastry blender or 2 forks, cut in butter and cream cheese until they resemble coarse crumbs. Add 1 cup cream to flour mixture, stirring until mixture is evenly moist. Working gently, bring mixture together with hands until a dough forms. (If dough seems dry and won't come together, add more cream, 1 tablespoon at a time.)
• Turn out dough onto a lightly floured surface, and knead gently until smooth by patting dough and folding it in half 5 to 7 times. Using a rolling pin, roll out dough to a ½-inch thickness. Using a 2-inch fluted round cutter dipped in flour, cut 18 scones from dough, rerolling scraps as necessary. Place scones 2 inches apart on prepared baking sheets.
• In a small bowl, whisk together remaining 2 tablespoons cream and remaining ¼ teaspoon cinnamon, remaining ¼ teaspoon cloves, remaining ¼ teaspoon allspice, remaining ¼ teaspoon nutmeg, and remaining ¼ teaspoon ginger. Brush tops of scones with cream mixture.
• Bake until edges of scones are golden brown and a wooden pick inserted in centers comes out clean, 12 to 15 minutes. Serve warm.

RECOMMENDED CONDIMENTS:
Devonshire Cream
Orange-Cranberry Marmalade

Rosemary-Fig Scones
MAKES 18

While at first blush, it might seem that the piney scent of rosemary might skew these scones toward the savory end of the flavor spectrum, in actuality, the evergreen herb just lends perfect balance to the sweetness of the granulated sugar and dried figs in the cake flour dough.

3 cups cake flour
½ cup granulated sugar
1 tablespoon baking powder
1 tablespoon chopped fresh rosemary
¼ teaspoon kosher salt
¼ teaspoon ground nutmeg
¾ cups frozen unsalted butter, coarsely grated
1 cup sliced dried black mission figs
¾ cup plus 1 tablespoon cold heavy whipping cream, divided
2 large eggs, divided

• Preheat oven to 400°. Line a rimmed baking sheet with parchment paper.
• In a large bowl, whisk together flour, sugar, baking powder, rosemary, salt, and nutmeg. Add cold butter, tossing until coated in flour mixture. Add figs, stirring until combined. Cover and freeze for 15 minutes.
• In a small bowl, whisk together ¾ cup cold cream and 1 egg. Add cream mixture to flour mixture, stirring until mixture is evenly moist and a dough forms.
• Turn out dough onto a lightly floured surface. Using well-floured hands, knead gently until smooth by patting dough and folding it in half 5 to 7 times. Using a rolling pin, roll out dough to ¾-inch thickness. Using a 2-inch fluted round cutter dipped in flour, cut 18 scones from dough, rerolling scraps only once. Place scones 2 inches apart on prepared baking sheet.
• In a small bowl, whisk together remaining 1 tablespoon cream and remaining 1 egg. Brush egg mixture onto tops of scones.
• Bake until edges of scones are golden brown and a wooden pick inserted in centers comes out clean, 12 to 15 minutes. Serve warm.

RECOMMENDED CONDIMENTS:
Devonshire Cream
Lemon Curd

White Chocolate–Peppermint Scones
MAKES 12

Crushed peppermint candies are right at home with white chocolate chips in these teatime treats that are perfect for a Christmas afternoon tea. For a festive presentation, garnish the platter with mint and sugared raspberries.

1¾ cups all-purpose flour
½ cup bread flour
¼ cup granulated sugar
1 tablespoon baking powder
¼ teaspoon kosher salt
⅛ teaspoon vanilla bean paste
6 tablespoons cold unsalted butter, cubed
½ cup white chocolate chips
1 tablespoon finely crushed peppermint candies
½ cup plus 2 tablespoons cold half-and-half, divided
1 large egg

• Preheat oven to 375°. Line a rimmed baking sheet with parchment paper.
• In a large bowl, whisk together both flours, sugar, baking powder, salt, and vanilla bean paste. Using a pastry blender or 2 forks, cut in cold butter until it resembles coarse crumbs. Add chocolate chips and peppermint candies, stirring until combined. Add ½ cup half-and-half, stirring until mixture is evenly moist. Working gently, bring mixture together with hands until a dough forms. (If dough seems dry and won't come together, add more half-and-half, 1 tablespoon at a time.)
• Turn out dough onto a lightly floured surface, and knead gently until smooth by patting dough and folding it in half 4 to 5 times. Using a rolling pin, roll out dough to a ½-inch thickness. Using a 2-inch fluted round cutter dipped in flour, cut 12 scones from dough, rerolling scraps as necessary.
• In a small bowl, whisk together egg and remaining 2 tablespoons half-and-half. Brush tops of scones with egg mixture. Freeze scones for 10 minutes.
• Bake until edges of scones are golden brown and a wooden pick inserted in centers comes out clean, approximately 16 minutes. Let cool slightly on a wire rack. Serve warm.

RECOMMENDED CONDIMENT:
Peppermint Cream (recipe follows)

Peppermint Cream
MAKES APPROXIMATELY 2 CUPS

This tasty candy-laced spread is a dessert in and of itself.

1 cup cold heavy whipping cream
1 teaspoon confectioners' sugar
1 teaspoon vanilla extract
1 tablespoon finely crushed peppermint candies, divided

• In a medium bowl, beat together cream, confectioners' sugar, and vanilla extract with a mixer at high speed until thickened and creamy. Cover, and refrigerate until needed, up to 2 hours.
• Just before serving, transfer cream to a serving bowl. Fold 1½ teaspoons peppermint candies into cream, and sprinkle remaining 1½ teaspoons peppermint candies over cream.

Raspberry-Mint Scones

MAKES 12

Fresh mint and tangy raspberries make an unexpected appearance in these delightful scones, which can be served as either a first or second course. Because fresh raspberries can be a little difficult to work with in scones, we opt here for freeze-dried berries.

2 cups all-purpose flour
⅓ cup granulated sugar
2 teaspoons baking powder
½ teaspoon fine sea salt
4 tablespoons cold unsalted butter, cubed
¾ cup freeze-dried raspberries
2 tablespoons finely chopped fresh mint
¾ cup plus 1 tablespoon cold heavy whipping cream,
    divided
½ teaspoon vanilla extract

• Preheat oven to 350°. Line a rimmed baking sheet with parchment paper.
• In a large bowl, whisk together flour, sugar, baking powder, and salt. Using a pastry blender or 2 forks, cut butter into flour mixture until it resembles coarse crumbs. Add raspberries and mint, stirring to blend.
• In a liquid-measuring cup, combine ¾ cup cream and vanilla extract, stirring to blend. Add to flour mixture, stirring to combine. Working gently, bring mixture together with hands until a dough forms. (If dough seems dry and won't come together, add more cream, 1 tablespoon at a time.)
• Turn out dough onto a lightly floured surface, and knead gently until smooth by patting dough and folding it in half 4 to 5 times. Using a rolling pin, roll dough to a 1-inch thickness. Using a 2-inch fluted round cutter dipped in flour, cut 12 scones from dough, rerolling scraps as necessary. Place scones 2 inches apart on prepared baking sheet.
• Brush tops of scones with remaining 1 tablespoon cream.
• Bake until edges of scones are golden brown and a wooden pick inserted in centers comes out clean, approximately 20 minutes. Serve warm.

RECOMMENDED CONDIMENTS:
Devonshire Cream
Lemon Curd

Hazelnut Scones
MAKES 10

Toasted hazelnuts permeate every morsel of these delightful pastries. For a truly decadent bite, serve with chocolate-hazelnut spread in addition to traditional Devonshire or clotted cream.

2 cups all-purpose flour
⅓ cup granulated sugar
2 teaspoons baking powder
½ teaspoon fine sea salt
4 tablespoons cold unsalted butter, cubed
⅓ cup chopped toasted hazelnuts
½ cup cold heavy whipping cream
¼ cup plus 3 tablespoons cold whole milk, divided
½ teaspoon vanilla extract
Garnish: blood orange slices

• Preheat oven to 350°. Line a rimmed baking sheet with parchment paper.
• In a large bowl, whisk together flour, sugar, baking powder, and salt. Using a pastry blender or 2 forks, cut butter into flour mixture until it resembles coarse crumbs. Add hazelnuts, stirring to combine.
• In a small bowl, whisk together cream, ¼ cup plus 2 tablespoons milk, and vanilla extract. Add to flour mixture, stirring until mixture comes together. Working gently, bring mixture together with hands until a dough forms. (If dough seems dry and won't come together, add more cream, 1 tablespoon at a time.)
• Turn out dough onto a lightly floured surface, and knead gently until smooth by patting dough and folding it in half 4 to 5 times. Using a rolling pin, roll out dough to a 1-inch thickness. Using a 2-inch fluted square cutter dipped in flour, cut 10 scones from dough, rerolling scraps as necessary. Place scones 2 inches apart on prepared baking sheet.
• Brush tops of scones with remaining 1 tablespoon milk.
• Bake until edges of scones are golden brown and a wooden pick inserted in centers comes out clean, approximately 20 minutes.
• Garnish with blood orange slices, if desired.

RECOMMENDED CONDIMENTS:
Devonshire Cream
Nutella Chocolate-Hazelnut Spread

6 tablespoons cold unsalted butter, cubed
½ cup finely chopped dried apricots
¼ cup finely chopped toasted walnuts
¾ cup plus 2 tablespoons cold heavy whipping cream, divided
1 large egg
¼ teaspoon vanilla bean paste

• Preheat oven to 375°. Line a rimmed baking sheet with parchment paper.
• In large bowl, whisk together both flours, brown sugar, baking powder, and salt. Using a pastry blender or 2 forks, cut in cold butter until it resembles coarse crumbs. Stir in apricots and walnuts.
• In a small bowl, whisk together ¾ cup cold cream, egg, and vanilla bean paste. Add cream mixture to flour mixture, stirring until mixture is evenly moist. Working gently, bring mixture together with hands until a dough forms. (If dough seems dry and won't come together, add more cream, 1 tablespoon at a time.)
• Turn out dough onto a lightly floured surface, and knead gently until smooth by patting dough and folding it in half 4 to 5 times. Using a rolling pin, roll out dough to a ½-inch thickness. Using a 2¼-inch fluted round cutter dipped in flour, cut 15 scones from dough, rerolling scraps as necessary. Place scones 1 inch apart on prepared baking sheet. Brush tops of scones with remaining 2 tablespoons cream.
• Bake until edges of scones are golden brown and a wooden pick inserted in centers comes out clean, 15 to 20 minutes. Serve warm.

RECOMMENDED CONDIMENTS:
Sweet Mascarpone Spread (recipe follows)
Peach-Amaretto Jam

Apricot-Walnut Scones
MAKES 15

Made with a combination of whole-wheat and all-purpose flours, these hearty, fruity scones feature vanilla bean paste. If you prefer to use vanilla extract instead, use the same amount as the recipe indicates for the paste.

2 cups all-purpose flour
¼ cup whole wheat flour
3 tablespoons firmly packed light brown sugar
2½ teaspoons baking powder
1 teaspoon kosher salt

Sweet Mascarpone Spread
MAKES ½ CUP

Mascarpone cheese alone is a perfect substitute for classic clotted cream, but when combined with heavy cream and confectioners' sugar, it makes for a truly luscious spread.

2 ounces mascarpone cheese
½ cup confectioners' sugar
½ cup cold heavy whipping cream

• In a small mixing bowl, beat together mascarpone cheese, sugar, and cream with a mixer at medium speed until light and creamy. Use immediately.

Lemon Scones

MAKES 12

*Lemonade and fresh lemon zest give these scones citrusy zip.
For festive flair, garnish the tops with rosemary sprigs and
curled lemon zest.*

1½ cup all-purpose flour
½ cup cake flour
2 tablespoons granulated sugar
2 teaspoons fresh lemon zest
1 teaspoon baking powder
½ teaspoon baking soda
½ teaspoon kosher salt
5 tablespoons cold unsalted butter, cubed
½ cup cold whole milk
¼ cup cold lemonade
1 large egg, beaten
¼ cup turbinado sugar
Garnish: rosemary sprigs and lemon zest curls

• Preheat oven to 375°. Line a rimmed baking sheet
with parchment paper.
• In a large bowl, whisk together both flours, granulated
sugar, lemon zest, baking powder, baking soda, and salt.
Using a pastry blender or 2 forks, cut in cold butter until
it resembles coarse crumbs.
• In a small bowl, stir together milk and lemonade.
Add milk mixture to flour mixture, stirring until mixture
is evenly moist. Working gently, bring mixture together
with hands until a dough forms. (If dough seems dry
and won't come together, add more milk, 1 tablespoon
at a time.)
• Turn out dough onto a lightly floured surface, and
knead gently until smooth by patting dough and folding
it in half 4 to 5 times. Using a rolling pin, roll out dough to
a ½-inch thickness. Using a 2-inch fluted round cutter,
cut 12 scones from dough, rerolling scraps as necessary.
Place scones 2 inches apart on prepared baking sheet.
• Brush tops of scones with egg, and sprinkle with
turbinado sugar.
• Bake until edges of scones are golden brown and
a wooden pick inserted in centers comes out clean,
12 to 15 minutes. Serve warm or at room temperature.
• Just before serving, garnish with rosemary sprigs
and lemon zest curls, if desired.

RECOMMENDED CONDIMENTS:
Devonshire Cream
Lemon Curd

Orange–Poppy Seed Gluten-free Scones
MAKES 12

Orange juice and zest give these scones a delightfully bright taste, which is further reinforced with the citrusy glaze.

2 cups gluten-free all-purpose flour*
¼ cup granulated sugar
2 tablespoons fresh orange zest
1 tablespoon baking powder
1½ teaspoons poppy seeds
½ teaspoon fine sea salt
5 tablespoons cold unsalted butter, cubed
¾ cup cold heavy whipping cream
¾ cup cold fresh orange juice, divided
1 large egg
1 tablespoon water
½ cup confectioners' sugar

• Preheat oven to 425°. Line a rimmed baking sheet with parchment paper.
• In a large bowl, whisk together flour, granulated sugar, orange zest, baking powder, poppy seeds, and salt. Using a pastry blender or 2 forks, cut in cold butter until it resembles coarse crumbs. Add cream and ¼ cup orange juice, stirring until combined. Working gently, bring mixture together with hands until a dough forms. (If dough seems dry and won't come together, add more cream, 1 tablespoon at a time.)
• Turn out dough onto a lightly floured* surface, and knead gently until smooth by patting dough and folding it in half 4 to 6 times. Using a rolling pin, roll out dough to a ¾-inch thickness. Using a 2¼-inch fluted square cutter dipped in flour*, cut 12 scones from dough, rerolling scraps as necessary. Place scones evenly spaced on prepared baking sheet.
• In a small bowl, whisk together egg and 1 tablespoon water. Brush tops of scones with egg wash.
• Bake until edges of scones are golden brown, 12 to 17 minutes. Let cool completely.
• Just before serving, in a small bowl, whisk together confectioners' sugar and remaining ½ cup orange juice until combined. Brush tops of scones with glaze.

We used King Arthur Gluten-Free Measure for Measure Flour.

Jasmine Green Tea–Coconut Gluten-free Scones

MAKES 14

The floral and fruity notes of litchi-flavored jasmine green tea pervade this gluten-free coconut scone. The recipe will work just as well with a standard jasmine green tea, too.

1½ cups plus 1 tablespoon heavy whipping cream, divided
5 tablespoons loose litchi-jasmine green tea leaves, divided
2¼ cups gluten-free all-purpose flour blend*
⅓ cup granulated sugar
1 tablespoon baking powder
½ teaspoon fine sea salt
6 tablespoons cold unsalted butter, cubed
⅓ cup minced dried unsweetened coconut
½ teaspoon coconut extract
¼ teaspoon vanilla extract

• In a medium saucepan, heat 1½ cups cream over medium-high heat until very hot but not boiling. Remove from heat; add 3 tablespoons tea leaves. Cover and let steep for 15 minutes. Strain cream mixture through a fine-mesh sieve into a heatproof container. Cover and refrigerate until cold, 6 to 8 hours.
• Preheat oven to 400°. Line a rimmed baking sheet with parchment paper.
• Using a mortar and pestle or an electric spice grinder, grind remaining 2 tablespoons tea leaves.
• In a large bowl, whisk together flour, sugar, baking powder, and salt. Using a pastry blender or 2 forks, cut in cold butter until it resembles coarse crumbs. Add coconut and ground tea leaves, stirring well.
• Add coconut extract and vanilla extract to cold steeped cream, stirring well. Add cream mixture to flour mixture, stirring until mixture is evenly moist. Working gently, bring mixture together with hands until a dough forms. (If dough seems dry and won't come together, add more cream, 1 tablespoon at a time.)

• Turn out dough onto a lightly floured* surface, and knead gently until smooth by patting dough and folding it in half 4 to 5 times. Using a rolling pin, roll out dough to a 1-inch thickness. Using a 2-inch fluted round cutter dipped in flour*, cut 14 scones from dough, rerolling scraps as necessary. Place scones 2 inches apart on prepared baking sheet.
• Brush top of scones with remaining 1 tablespoon cream.
• Bake until edges of scones are golden brown and a wooden pick inserted in centers comes out clean, approximately 13 minutes. Serve warm.

We recommend King Arthur's Gluten-Free Measure for Measure Flour or Bob's Red Mill Gluten Free 1-to-1 Baking Flour.

RECOMMENDED CONDIMENTS:
Devonshire Cream
Pineapple Preserves

USING CONVENTIONAL FLOUR INSTEAD OF GLUTEN-FREE FLOUR

Replace gluten-free flour with an equal amount of all-purpose flour, and follow the recipe, but only add enough of the cream mixture for a dough to begin to form. (If dough is too wet, scones will spread out instead of rising properly.) Since conventional flour has gluten, be sure to handle the dough gently, or the scones will be tough. Bake as indicated in the recipe.

Savories

Grape & Gorgonzola Tea Sandwiches

MAKES 8

Flower-shaped marbled bread slices are perfect for a springtime or summertime sandwich filled with red grape slices and a delightful Gorgonzola and sour cream spread as well as spring mix lettuces dressed with a Champagne vinaigrette.

8 slices rye and pumpernickel swirl bread, frozen
2¼ teaspoons raspberry Champagne vinegar
1½ teaspoons extra-virgin olive oil
⅛ teaspoon kosher salt
⅛ teaspoon ground black pepper
1 cup spring mix lettuces
2 tablespoons Gorgonzola cheese
2 tablespoons sour cream
1 cup seedless red grapes, cut into ⅛-inch-thick slices
Garnish: sliced seedless red grapes

• Using a 2-inch flower-shaped cutter, cut 16 shapes from frozen bread slices. To prevent drying out, place bread shapes in a resealable plastic bag to thaw.
• In a medium bowl, whisk together vinegar, oil, salt, and pepper. Add lettuces, tossing to coat.
• In a small bowl, beat together Gorgonzola cheese and sour cream with a mixer at medium speed until smooth.
• Spread a layer of cheese mixture onto each bread shape. Arrange lettuce mixture on 8 bread shapes. Top with a single layer of grape slices, arranging so grapes are in line with the curves of the bread flowers. Cover with remaining bread shapes to make 8 sandwiches. Serve immediately, or cover with damp paper towels, place in an airtight container, and refrigerate until serving time.
• Garnish with sliced grapes, if desired.

Smoked Chicken & Avocado Tea Sandwiches
MAKES 12

Toasted whole-wheat bread holds the smoky goodness of deli chicken and a paprika spread. Add to that fresh tomato, avocado, and watercress for a refreshingly light tea sandwich.

2 tablespoons ketchup
2 tablespoons mayonnaise
½ teaspoon smoked paprika
8 slices whole-wheat bread, toasted
6 ounces thinly sliced deli smoked chicken
½ cup thinly sliced grape tomatoes
½ cup watercress
½ small ripe avocado, cut into 8 (⅛-inch-thick) slices*
Garnish: watercress

• In a small bowl, whisk together ketchup, mayonnaise, and paprika. Spread a layer of ketchup mixture onto each bread slice.
• Arrange chicken on 4 bread slices. Top with tomato slices, watercress, and 2 avocado slices each. Cover with remaining bread slices, spread side down.
• Using a serrated bread knife in a gentle sawing motion, trim and discard crusts from sandwiches. Cut each sandwich into 3 (3x1-inch) rectangles. Serve immediately, or place in an airtight container and refrigerate until serving time.
• Garnish with watercress, if desired.

*Because avocado will turn brown if not used promptly, we recommend gently tossing slices in lemon juice or lime juice, if necessary.

Apricot, Bacon & Brie Phyllo Tartlets
MAKES 15

These sweet and savory morsels are easy to make and so delicious, whether served warm or at room temperature, that you might just want to double the recipe.

4 slices bacon
¼ cup apricot preserves
1 tablespoon apple cider vinegar
15 frozen mini phyllo cups, thawed
½ cup spreadable Brie cheese
Garnish: fresh thyme

• In a medium skillet, cook bacon over medium heat until crisp. Remove bacon, and let drain on paper towels. Let cool. Using a sharp knife, finely chop bacon.
• In a small saucepan, stir together preserves and vinegar over medium heat until well combined. Add bacon, and bring mixture to a rolling boil. Reduce heat to low; simmer for 5 to 6 minutes. Remove from heat.
• Preheat oven to 350°. Line a rimmed baking sheet with parchment paper.
• Fill each phyllo cup with 1½ teaspoons Brie cheese. Top each with ½ teaspoon bacon mixture. Place tartlets 2 inches apart on prepared baking sheet.
• Bake for 10 minutes. Serve warm or at room temperature.
• Garnish with thyme, if desired.

Turkey & Mushroom Phyllo Cups
MAKES 15

A rich filling of turkey, prosciutto, and mushrooms hides under a cheese-topped slice of cherry tomato. Choose seasonally appropriate cutters for the cheese shapes if serving these delicious morsels for occasions other than Christmas.

15 frozen mini phyllo cups, thawed
2 tablespoons unsalted butter
1 tablespoon sliced shallot
8 ounces whole white button mushrooms, sliced
¼ cup finely chopped roast deli turkey
3 tablespoons finely chopped prosciutto
1 tablespoon finely snipped fresh chives
2 tablespoons mayonnaise
2 tablespoons Dijon mustard
3 slices provolone cheese
15 slices cherry tomato
Garnish: ground paprika and fresh chives

• Preheat oven to 350°. Line a rimmed baking sheet with parchment paper.
• Arrange phyllo cups on prepared baking sheet.
• In a medium sauté pan, melt butter over medium heat. Add shallot and mushrooms, cooking, stirring constantly, until tender, approximately 5 minutes. Let mixture cool to room temperature. Using a sharp knife, finely chop cooked mushroom mixture.
• In a medium bowl, stir together mushroom mixture, turkey, prosciutto, and chives.
• In a small bowl, stir together mayonnaise and mustard.
• Using a 1-inch Christmas tree–shaped linzer cutter, cut 15 shapes from cheese slices.
• Divide mayonnaise mixture among phyllo cups. Fill phyllo cups with mushroom mixture. Place a tomato slice on top of mushroom mixture. Top with a cheese cutout.
• Bake until cheese is warm and shiny, approximately 3 minutes.
• Garnish with paprika and chives, if desired. Serve immediately.

MAKE-AHEAD TIP: Mushroom mixture can be made a day in advance, stored in a covered container, and refrigerated. Reheat gently in a sauté pan before using.

Pomegranate-Beef Flatbreads
MAKES 16

Simple, yet upscale, these eye-catching canapés, featuring slices of pomegranate molasses–coated beef filets as well as pomegranate arils and peppery arugula, will delight the taste buds.

2 (6- to 8-ounce) beef filets mignons
1 tablespoon plus 1 teaspoon olive oil, divided
¼ teaspoon garlic salt
¼ teaspoon ground coriander
¼ teaspoon ground black pepper
2 tablespoons pomegranate molasses*
2 naan flatbreads
1 tablespoon salted butter, melted
½ cup pomegranate arils
16 sprigs baby arugula
Garnish: pomegranate molasses

• Preheat oven to 350°. Line a rimmed baking sheet with foil. Line a second rimmed baking sheet with parchment paper.
• Rub beef filets with 1 tablespoon oil, and sprinkle with garlic salt, coriander, and pepper, covering all sides. Let stand at room temperature for 15 minutes.
• In a medium sauté pan, heat remaining 1 teaspoon oil over medium-high heat. Add filets, and reduce heat to medium; cook until seared, approximately 3 minutes per side. Place seared filets on foil-lined baking sheet.
• Bake for 8 to 10 minutes. (Filets will be medium-rare.) Brush filets with pomegranate molasses. Let cool to room temperature.
• Using a sharp knife, cut filets into 16 thin slices.
• Using a 2½-inch triangular cutter, cut 16 shapes from naan flatbreads. Brush tops of bread triangles with melted butter. Place bread triangles on parchment paper–lined baking sheet.
• Bake until warm and slightly crisp, 8 to 10 minutes. Remove from oven, and let cool completely.
• Place a filet slice on each bread triangle. Top with pomegranate arils and arugula.
• Garnish with a drizzle of pomegranate molasses just before serving, if desired. Serve immediately.

*We used Al Wadi Pomegranate Molasses, available at Whole Foods and other specialty grocers.

Crab & Cucumber Tea Sandwiches
MAKES 9

Tarragon and roasted red pepper add color and flavor to lump crabmeat in these tea sandwiches that are perfect for the holiday season and beyond.

2 (8-ounce) containers jumbo lump crabmeat,
    picked free of shell
1 teaspoon chopped fresh tarragon
1 tablespoon chopped roasted red pepper
Tarragon-Champagne Vinaigrette (recipe follows)
6 large slices firm white sandwich bread
2 tablespoons mayonnaise
27 thin slices English cucumber
Garnish: fresh tarragon sprigs and roasted red pepper

• In the work bowl of a food processor, pulse crabmeat a few times to break up jumbo lumps.
• In a medium bowl, toss crab with tarragon and roasted red pepper. Add enough vinaigrette to moisten.
• Using a serrated bread knife in a gentle sawing motion, cut bread slices into 3¾x3-inch rectangles, discarding crusts. Cut each bread rectangle into 3 (3x1¼-inch) rectangles.
• Spread a layer of mayonnaise onto each bread rectangle. Arrange 3 cucumber slices each on mayonnaise side of 9 bread rectangles. Spread an even layer of crab salad over cucumbers. Top with remaining bread rectangles, mayonnaise side down.

• Garnish with fresh tarragon sprigs and chopped roasted red pepper, if desired.

MAKE-AHEAD TIP: Sandwiches can be made a few hours in advance, covered with damp paper towels, stored in an airtight container, and refrigerated. Garnish just before serving.

Tarragon-Champagne Vinaigrette
MAKES ¾ CUP

Rather than relying on fresh tarragon, this vinaigrette gets its slightly licorice, herbaceous flavor from tarragon-infused Champagne vinegar, which is available at most grocery stores.

½ cup avocado oil
¼ cup tarragon Champagne vinegar
1 teaspoon granulated sugar
1 teaspoon finely chopped shallot
½ teaspoon fine sea salt
¼ teaspoon ground black pepper

• In a screw-top glass jar, shake together all ingredients until emulsified. Let stand for flavors to meld, approximately 1 hour. Shake again before using.

MAKE-AHEAD TIP: Vinaigrette can be made a day in advance and refrigerated. Let come to room temperature before using, and shake again.

Smoked Trout Toasts with Pickled Red Onion

MAKES 24

Herb-laced cream cheese sits on toasted pumpernickle triangles and is topped with smoked trout and pickled red onion.

¼ cup (⅛-inch) sliced red onion
¼ cup white wine vinegar
¼ cup water
1½ tablespoons granulated sugar
½ teaspoon fine sea salt
¼ teaspoon coriander seeds
6 slices Jewish rye pumpernickel bread
1 tablespoon unsalted butter, melted
4 ounces cream cheese, softened
4 teaspoons finely chopped fresh dill
2 teaspoons finely chopped fresh chives
1 ounce skinless smoked trout cut into 24 (¾-inch)
    pieces, pin bones removed
Garnish: fresh dill fronds

• Place onion in a small heatproof bowl.
• In a small saucepan, bring vinegar, ¼ cup water, sugar, salt, and coriander seeds to a boil together over medium-high heat. Cook for 2 minutes, stirring occasionally. Remove from heat, and pour over onion. Let cool for 30 minutes. Transfer mixture to an airtight container, and refrigerate until needed, up to a day.
• Preheat oven to 350°. Line a rimmed baking sheet with parchment paper.
• Using a serrated bread knife in a gentle sawing motion, cut each bread slice into a 4x2-inch rectangle. Cut rectangles in half, creating 2 (2-inch) squares. Cut each square in half diagonally, creating 2 triangles. Place bread triangles on prepared baking sheet. Brush with melted butter.
• Bake until bread is crisp, 7 to 10 minutes. Let cool completely.
• In a small bowl, stir together cream cheese, dill, and chives until well combined. Transfer mixture to a piping bag fitted with a ¼-inch round piping tip (Ateco #802). Pipe approximately ½ teaspoon cream cheese mixture onto each toast. Top with 1 trout piece and 1 onion slice. (Reserve remaining onion for another use.)
• Garnish with dill fronds, if desired. Serve immediately.

MAKE-AHEAD TIP: Bread triangles can be prepared several hours in advance, cooled, and stored at room temperature in an airtight container until needed.

sandwich into 2 (2x1½-inch) rectangles. Serve immediately, or cover with damp paper towels, place in an
airtight container, and refrigerate until serving time.
Just before serving, garnish with arugula, if desired.

Sweet Potato Canapés
MAKES 24

Crispy sweet potato slices support layers of creamy
fontina cheese, fresh pear, and spicy candied walnuts.

2 tablespoons extra-virgin olive oil, divided
1 tablespoon cane syrup, divided
¼ teaspoon kosher salt, divided
¼ teaspoon ground black pepper, divided
1 large sweet potato, peeled
½ cup finely chopped walnuts
3 large Bosc pears, peeled
2 ounces fontina cheese
Garnish: fresh thyme sprigs

• Preheat oven to 250°. Line 2 rimmed baking sheets
with parchment paper.
• In a medium bowl, whisk together 1 tablespoon olive
oil, ½ tablespoon cane syrup, ⅛ teaspoon salt, and
⅛ teaspoon pepper.
• Using the third setting on a French mandoline, thinly
slice sweet potato to create round discs. Arrange sweet
potato slices ¼-inch apart on prepared baking sheets.
Brush tops of sweet potato slices with olive oil mixture.
• Bake until sweet potato slices are dried out and crisp,
approximately 55 minutes. Flip slices over, and press
down to flatten. Bake an additional 35 minutes. Store
in an airtight container until ready to use, up to a day.
• Increase oven temperature to 350°. Line another
rimmed baking sheet with parchment paper.
• In a medium bowl, whisk together remaining 1 tablespoon olive oil, remaining ½ tablespoon cane syrup,
remaining ⅛ teaspoon salt, and remaining ⅛ teaspoon
pepper. Add walnuts, stirring well. Transfer walnuts to
prepared baking sheet.
• Bake for 8 minutes. Let cool completely.
• Using a sharp knife, cut ¼-inch-thick slices from
pears. Using a ½-inch round cutter, cut 24 rounds from
pear slices, discarding scraps.
• Gently spread a thin layer of fontina cheese onto each
sweet potato slice. Top each with a pear round. Sprinkle
each with ¼ teaspoon walnuts.
• Garnish with a thyme sprig, if desired. Serve immediately.

Shrimp Tea Sandwiches
MAKES 10

Seafood lovers will appreciate this classic sandwich, whose flavor
is enhanced with smoked paprika, lime juice, and a little garlic.

½ cup mayonnaise
1 teaspoon kosher salt
½ teaspoon smoked paprika
¼ teaspoon ground black pepper
1 pound jumbo shrimp, peeled, deveined, and cooked
¼ cup fresh lime juice
½ teaspoon minced garlic
1 cup arugula
15 very thin slices wheat bread
Garnish: arugula

• In a medium bowl, whisk together mayonnaise, salt,
paprika, and pepper.
• In a food processor, pulse together shrimp, lime juice,
and garlic until shrimp is finely chopped. Transfer to a
medium bowl. Add mayonnaise mixture, stirring until
combined.
• Spread 2 tablespoons shrimp mixture each onto
10 bread slices. Top shrimp layer evenly with arugula.
Stack bread slices in pairs, shrimp and arugula side up.
Cover each with a plain bread slice to create 5 triple-
stack sandwiches.
• Using a serrated bread knife in a gentle sawing motion,
trim and discard crusts from sandwiches. Cut each

Savory Goat Cheese Cheesecakes with Red Onion Jam

MAKES 12

Made-from-scratch Red Onion Jam tops these fluffy, savory cheesecakes that perch prettily on cornmeal crusts.

½ cup plus 2 tablespoons all-purpose flour, divided
¼ cup cornmeal
5 tablespoons unsalted butter, melted
2⅛ teaspoons kosher salt, divided
¾ teaspoon ground black pepper, divided
12 ounces cream cheese, room temperature
2 ounces goat cheese, room temperature
⅓ cup crème fraîche, room temperature
1 large egg, room temperature
1 large egg yolk, room temperature
Red Onion Jam (recipe follows)
Garnish: fresh oregano sprigs

• Preheat oven to 350°. Spray a 12-well removable-bottom mini cheesecake pan with cooking spray.
• In a small bowl, stir together ½ cup flour, cornmeal, melted butter, 2 teaspoons salt, and ½ teaspoon pepper. Divide mixture among wells of prepared pan, pressing into bottoms to form level crusts.
• Bake until crusts are golden brown, approximately 15 minutes.
• Reduce oven temperature to 325°.
• In a large bowl, beat together cream cheese, goat cheese, and remaining 2 tablespoons flour with a mixer at medium speed until well combined. Add crème fraîche, beating until incorporated. Add egg, egg yolk, remaining ⅛ teaspoon salt, and remaining ¼ teaspoon pepper, beating at low speed until combined. Using a levered 3-tablespoon scoop, divide batter among wells of prepared pan.
• Bake until edges of cheesecakes are set, 35 to 40 minutes. Let cool completely in pan. Gently run a thin knife around each cheesecake to release sides from pan. Refrigerate cheesecakes until set, at least 4 hours or overnight.
• Carefully remove chilled cheesecakes from pan by pushing up on bottom discs. Using an offset spatula, remove each cheesecake from metal disc and place on a serving platter. Spoon Red Onion Jam over tops of cheesecakes.
• Garnish with oregano, if desired. Serve cold or at room temperature.

Red Onion Jam

MAKES 1 CUP

Red wine and balsamic vinegar give this savory jam a hint of sweetness. The perfect topper for Savory Goat Cheese Cheese-cakes, it also would make for a tasty sandwich spread.

1 cup finely diced red onion
¼ cup finely diced shallots
½ teaspoon kosher salt
½ cup dry red wine
3 ounces liquid fruit pectin*
2 tablespoons aged balsamic vinegar
1 tablespoon fresh lemon juice

• In a medium saucepan, bring onion, shallots, salt, wine, pectin, vinegar, and lemon juice to a boil together over medium-high heat. Reduce to a simmer, and cook, stirring occasionally, for 20 minutes.
• Transfer jam to a large heatproof bowl. Let cool completely. Store jam in an airtight container and refrigerate until needed, up to 3 days.

We used Sure-Jell Liquid Pectin.

- Using a serrated bread knife in a gentle sawing motion, trim and discard crusts from sandwiches. Cut each sandwich in half diagonally, creating 2 triangles. Serve immediately, or cover with damp paper towels, place in a covered container, and refrigerate until serving time.
- Just before serving, garnish with arugula and toasted pine nuts, if desired.

Zucchini & Bacon–Filled Mushrooms
MAKES 64

These flavor-packed button mushrooms are bound to be a teatime favorite for any guests who follow a gluten-free diet and even those who don't. Stuffed with a mixture of bacon, zucchini, ricotta cheese, and onion, these savory morsels are oh-so tasty.

3 slices thick-cut bacon
2 cups diced zucchini
½ cup diced fresh button mushrooms
2 tablespoons diced onion
4 tablespoons olive oil, divided
1 teaspoon minced garlic, divided
½ teaspoon kosher salt
¼ teaspoon ground black pepper
¼ cup ricotta cheese
64 fresh button mushrooms, stemmed
Garnish: chervil

- Preheat oven to 425°. Line a rimmed baking sheet with parchment paper.
- In a large skillet, cook bacon over medium heat until crisp, approximately 10 minutes. Remove bacon, and let drain on paper towels, reserving drippings in skillet. Let bacon cool; roughly chop, and set aside.
- Add zucchini, diced mushrooms, onion, 1 tablespoon oil, ¼ teaspoon garlic, salt, and pepper to bacon drippings in skillet, stirring to coat. Cook over medium heat until mushrooms and zucchini begin to wilt, approximately 5 minutes. Remove from heat; transfer to a large heatproof bowl. Add bacon and ricotta, stirring until combined.
- In another large bowl, toss together stemmed mushrooms, remaining 3 tablespoons oil, and remaining ¾ teaspoon garlic. Place mushrooms, stem side down, on prepared baking sheet.
- Bake for 15 minutes. Turn mushrooms over, and spoon ½ teaspoon filling into each mushroom. Bake for 5 minutes more. Serve warm.
- Garnish with chervil, if desired.

Ham Tea Sandwiches with Pine Nut Spread
MAKES 12

Unlike salty country ham, Virginia ham is sweet, having been smoked with a mixture of apple and hickory woods. Here, it is paired with a sandwich spread made with fontina cheese, mustard, and pine nuts.

4 ounces fontina cheese
2 tablespoons pine nuts, toasted
1 tablespoon Dijon mustard
12 very thin slices white bread
1 cup arugula
½ pound thinly sliced Virginia ham
Garnish: arugula and toasted pine nuts

- In the work bowl of a food processor, pulse together fontina cheese, pine nuts, and mustard until combined and smooth. Spread an even layer of pine nut spread on 6 bread slices. Set aside.
- Divide arugula among remaining 6 bread slices. Layer 2 ham slices over arugula on each bread slice. Top each with a reserved bread slice, pine nut spread side down to make 6 sandwiches.

Savory Mushroom Cheesecakes
MAKES 25 SERVINGS

Warm, savory cheesecake squares topped with gourmet mushrooms will be an unexpected, yet decadent, addition to any tiered tray for afternoon tea.

1¾ cups finely chopped toasted pecans
1¾ cups crumbled buttery round crackers
6 tablespoons unsalted butter, melted
1 large egg white
10 ounces goat cheese, softened

1 (8-ounce) package cream cheese, softened
1½ cups heavy whipping cream
3 large eggs, room temperature
2 cups grated Swiss cheese
1 tablespoon all-purpose flour
¾ teaspoon kosher salt, divided
½ teaspoon ground black pepper, divided
1½ tablespoons olive oil
1½ tablespoons unsalted butter
1½ cups gourmet blend mushrooms, trimmed
2 teaspoons chopped fresh thyme
Garnish: fresh thyme sprigs

• Preheat oven to 325°. Spray a 9-inch square cake pan with cooking spray. Line pan with parchment paper, letting excess extend over sides of pan.
• In a medium bowl, stir together pecans, crackers, melted butter, and egg white until combined. Press mixture into bottom of prepared pan.
• Bake for 10 minutes. Let cool completely on a wire rack.
• In a large bowl, beat together goat cheese and cream cheese with a mixer at medium speed until smooth. Scrape sides of bowl. Add cream, beating to combine. Add eggs, one at a time, beating well after each addition. Scrape sides of bowl. Add Swiss cheese, flour, ½ tea-spoon salt, and ¼ teaspoon pepper, beating to combine. Pour batter into prepared crust, smoothing top with an offset spatula.
• Bake cheesecake until set, approximately 40 minutes. Let cool in pan for 30 minutes. Refrigerate for at least 2 hours.
• Preheat oven to 350°. Line a rimmed baking sheet with parchment paper.
• Run a long knife between cake pan and parchment paper. Using excess parchment as handles, remove cheesecake from pan, and place on a cutting board. Using a sharp knife, trim edges of cake. Cut into 25 (1¾-inch) squares, cleaning knife between cuts. Place on prepared baking sheet.
• Bake cheesecake squares until warmed, 5 to 8 minutes.
• Meanwhile, in a medium nonstick skillet, heat oil and butter over medium-high heat. Add mushrooms, thyme, remaining ¼ teaspoon salt, and remaining ¼ teaspoon pepper; cook for 5 minutes without stirring. Stir mush-rooms to sear on all sides. Remove from pan, and let drain on paper towels. Top warm cheesecake squares with hot mushrooms.
• Garnish with thyme, if desired. Serve immediately.

Turkey & Stuffing Canapés
MAKES 32

Turkey and stuffing get a tea-appropriate remake in these delectable canapés that are topped with a peppery, yet maple-sweet, crème fraîche and garnished with a tiny sage leaf.

½ pound loaf crusty white bread, cut into ½-inch
    cubes
¼ cup unsalted butter
1 cup chopped yellow onion
1 cup chopped celery
1¼ cups low-sodium chicken broth
2 large eggs, lightly beaten
1½ tablespoons finely chopped fresh parsley
1½ tablespoons finely chopped fresh sage
1 tablespoon finely chopped fresh rosemary
1 teaspoon kosher salt
½ teaspoon ground black pepper
½ pound thinly sliced oven-roasted turkey breast
Pepper & Maple Crème Fraîche (recipe follows)
Garnish: fresh sage leaves

- Preheat oven to 250°.
- Spread bread cubes in a single layer on a rimmed baking sheet. Bake until bread is dried out, approximately 1 hour. Let cool on a wire rack.
- Increase oven temperature to 350°. Spray 32 wells of 2 (24-well) mini muffin pans with cooking spray.
- In a large sauté pan, melt butter over medium-high heat. Add onion and celery, cooking until tender, stirring occasionally, approximately 15 minutes.
- In a large bowl, stir together baked bread cubes, onion mixture, broth, eggs, parsley, sage, rosemary, salt, and pepper. Using a levered 2-tablespoon scoop, divide stuffing mixture among prepared wells of muffin pans. Using the back of the scoop, smooth stuffing mixture to create an even surface.
- Cover muffin pans with foil, and bake for 20 minutes. Uncover, and bake until lightly browned, 20 to 25 minutes. Let cool slightly before removing from muffin pans.
- Place Pepper & Maple Crème Fraîche in a piping bag fitted with a small round tip (Wilton #2A). Pipe a dot on each stuffing canapé.
- Using a 1¼-inch round cutter, cut 32 rounds from turkey slices. Cover crème fraîche dot on each stuffing canapé with a turkey round.
- Pipe a dot of crème fraîche on each turkey round.
- Garnish with sage, if desired. Serve immediately.

MAKE-AHEAD TIP: Bread cubes can be baked a day ahead, cooled completely, and stored in an airtight container. Turkey rounds can be prepared a day ahead, stored in an airtight container, and refrigerated until needed.

Pepper & Maple Crème Fraîche
MAKES ½ CUP

A little maple syrup and dashes of salt and pepper transform tangy crème fraîche into a memorable topping.

1 (4-ounce) container crème fraîche
1 teaspoon maple syrup
⅛ teaspoon kosher salt
⅛ teaspoon ground black pepper

- In a small bowl, whisk together crème fraîche, syrup, salt, and pepper until well combined and thickened. Use immediately, or cover and refrigerate for up to a day.

Sweets

Tea-Infused Tartlets with Fresh Fruit

MAKES 8

Coconut-scented green tea infuses delicious flavor to the pastry cream filling of these colorful tartlets.

1½ cups granulated sugar
1½ cups half-and-half
2 tea bags coconut green tea blend*
½ teaspoon vanilla bean paste**
6 large egg yolks
2 teaspoons cornstarch
1 (14.1-ounce) package refrigerated piecrust dough
    (2 sheets)
¼ cup sliced fresh strawberries
¼ cup halved pitted fresh Bing cherries
2 tablespoons pomegranate arils
Garnish: fresh mint leaves

• In a medium saucepan, combine sugar, half-and-half, tea bags, and vanilla bean paste. Cook over medium heat just until mixture begins to boil. Remove from heat; let steep for 5 minutes. Discard tea bags.
• In a medium bowl, whisk together egg yolks and cornstarch until smooth. Using a ladle, pour 1 cup hot cream mixture into egg mixture in a slow, steady stream, whisking constantly. Return mixture to saucepan and bring to a boil, whisking constantly. Cook over medium heat, stirring constantly, until thickened. Transfer pastry cream to a medium heatproof bowl. Cover with a piece of plastic wrap, pressing wrap directly onto surface of pastry cream to prevent a skin from forming. Once pastry cream cools, refrigerate until chilled, approximately 2 hours.
• Preheat oven to 400°. Line a rimmed baking sheet with parchment paper.
• On a lightly floured surface, unroll each dough sheet. Using a 4½-inch round cutter, cut 8 rounds from dough, discarding scraps. (See how-to on page 129.) Transfer rounds to 8 (3¾-inch) fluted round removable-bottom tartlet pans, pressing into bottom and up sides. Using large end of a chopstick, press dough into indentations in sides of tartlet pans. Place tartlet pans on prepared baking sheet. Prick bottom of tartlet dough 3 times with a fork. Freeze until firm, approximately 20 minutes.
• Top each tartlet pan with a parchment paper square, letting ends extend over edges of pans. Gently add pie weights or dried beans.
• Bake for 8 minutes. Carefully remove parchment paper and weights. Bake until golden brown, approximately 5 minutes more. Let cool completely on wire racks.
• Just before serving, gently remove tartlet shells from tartlet pans. Divide pastry cream among tartlet shells, smoothing tops with an offset spatula. Arrange strawberries, cherries, and pomegranate arils atop pastry cream.
• Garnish with mint, if desired. Serve immediately.

We used Harney & Sons Bangkok green tea blend, available at harney.com or by calling 800-832-8463.
**If vanilla bean paste is not available, substitute an equal amount of pure vanilla extract.*

Chocolate-Rosemary Shortbread Cookies

MAKES 84

Guests will want more than one of these herbaceous, chocolaty shortbread cookies, topped with a layer of Pink Grapefruit Glaze.

1 cup unsalted butter, softened
¾ cup confectioners' sugar
2 ounces semisweet baking chocolate, melted
    according to package instructions
½ teaspoon vanilla extract
2 cups all-purpose flour
3 tablespoons unsweetened cocoa powder
½ teaspoon baking powder
¼ teaspoon kosher salt
1 tablespoon chopped fresh rosemary
Pink Grapefruit Glaze (recipe follows)
Garnish: fresh rosemary sprigs

• In a large bowl, beat together butter and confectioners' sugar with a mixer at medium speed until creamy. Add melted chocolate, beating until combined. Beat in vanilla extract until combined. Scrape sides of bowl.
• In a medium bowl, sift together flour, cocoa powder, baking powder, and salt. Stir in rosemary. With mixer at low speed, gradually add flour mixture to butter mixture, beating until combined. Shape dough into a disk, and wrap in plastic wrap. Refrigerate for at least 1 hour.
• Preheat oven to 350°. Line several rimmed baking sheets with parchment paper.
• Using a rolling pin, roll out dough to a ¼-inch thickness on a lightly floured surface. Using a 1½-inch fluted round cutter, cut as many cookies as possible from dough, rerolling scraps only twice. Place cookies on prepared baking sheets.
• Bake for 8 minutes. Let cool completely on wire racks.
• Spread Pink Grapefruit Glaze onto cookies. While glaze is still wet, garnish with rosemary sprigs, if desired. Let glaze set for 1 hour before serving or packaging. Store between layers of wax paper in an airtight container at room temperature for up to a day.

Pink Grapefruit Glaze

MAKES APPROXIMATELY ⅓ CUP

Pink grapefruit offers a bright, tart flavor profile for this sweet glaze.

1½ cups confectioners' sugar
1 tablespoon fresh
    pink grapefruit zest
3 tablespoons fresh
    pink grapefruit juice

• In a small bowl, whisk together confectioners' sugar, zest, and juice until smooth. Use immediately.

Strawberry Tartlets with Vanilla-Citrus Custard

MAKES 20

Traditional strawberry tartlets get a fresh, dainty look in these petite versions that feature a flat almond crust attractively piped with a border of Vanilla-Citrus Custard and set with an upright, hulled strawberry in the center.

¾ cup unsalted butter, softened
1 cup confectioners' sugar
1 large egg
1½ cups all-purpose flour
1¼ cups almond flour
1 cup chopped roasted almonds
½ teaspoon kosher salt
Vanilla-Citrus Custard (recipe follows)
20 fresh strawberries, hulled

• Line a 9-inch square baking pan with plastic wrap.
• In a large bowl, beat together butter and confectioners' sugar with a mixer at medium speed until fluffy, 3 to 4 minutes, stopping to scrape sides of bowl. Add egg, beating to combine.
• In a medium bowl, whisk together both flours, almonds, and salt. With mixer at low speed, gradually add flour mixture to butter mixture, beating just until combined. Press dough into bottom of prepared pan. Cover with plastic wrap, and refrigerate for 1 hour.
• Preheat oven to 350°. Line 2 rimmed baking sheets with parchment paper.
• Turn out dough onto a lightly floured surface. Using a rolling pin, roll out dough to a ¼-inch thickness. Using a 2¼-inch round cutter, cut 20 rounds from dough. Place rounds on prepared baking sheets. Using a fork, poke several holes in dough rounds.
• Bake until edges are just beginning to brown, approximately 10 minutes. Let cool completely on wire racks.
• Place Vanilla-Citrus Custard in a large piping bag fitted with a rose-shaped tip (Wilton #125). Pipe custard into center of tartlet shell rounds, and create a ribbon design around edge of each shell. Place a strawberry upright in center of each tartlet.

MAKE-AHEAD TIP: Tartlet shells can be made 3 days in advance and stored in an airtight container.

Vanilla-Citrus Custard

MAKES 2¾ CUPS

This egg-based custard flavored with the zests of lemon and orange as well as with vanilla bean paste is good enough to eat on its own. If vanilla bean paste is not available, replace it in equal portions with pure vanilla extract.

1½ cups heavy whipping cream
¾ cup whole milk
2 large egg yolks
1 large egg
⅓ cup firmly packed light brown sugar
¼ cup plus ½ tablespoon cornstarch
½ teaspoon fresh lemon zest
½ teaspoon fresh orange zest
½ teaspoon vanilla bean paste
1 tablespoon unsalted butter, softened

• In a medium saucepan, bring cream and milk to a boil together over medium heat.
• In a medium bowl, whisk together egg yolks, egg, brown sugar, cornstarch, lemon zest, orange zest, and vanilla bean paste. Whisking constantly, slowly add hot cream mixture to egg mixture. Return cream mixture to saucepan, and cook, whisking constantly, until thickened.
• Transfer custard to a medium bowl. Add butter, stirring until incorporated. Cover with a piece of plastic wrap, pressing wrap directly onto surface of custard to prevent a skin from forming. Refrigerate for 1 hour before using.

Lavender, Mango & Peach Macarons
MAKES 36

French macarons, classic meringue-based sandwich cookies, are elevated when infused with the floral taste of lavender and filled with a creamy mango-peach mixture.

½ cup egg whites (approximately 4 egg whites), divided
1⅓ cups confectioners' sugar
1¼ cups almond flour
½ teaspoon food-grade lavender flavoring*
⅛ teaspoon violet gel food coloring*
½ cup plus 6½ teaspoons granulated sugar
3 tablespoons water
½ teaspoon meringue powder
Fruity & Floral Filling (recipe follows)

• Place egg whites in a large bowl, and let stand at room temperature for exactly 3 hours. (Aging egg whites in this manner is essential to creating the perfect macaron.)
• Line 2 rimmed baking sheets with parchment paper. Using a pencil, draw 72 (1½-inch) circles 2 inches apart onto parchment; turn parchment over.
• In a medium bowl, sift together confectioners' sugar and almond flour. Add ¼ cup egg whites, lavender flavoring, and food coloring, stirring gently to combine.
• In a small saucepan, bring granulated sugar and 3 tablespoons water to a boil over medium-high heat. Cook until mixture registers 248° on a candy thermometer, approximately 5 minutes.
• Meanwhile, in the bowl of a stand mixer fitted with the whisk attachment, beat together meringue powder and remaining ¼ cup egg whites at low speed until foamy. Increase mixer speed to high. Add hot sugar syrup in a slow, steady stream, being careful not to hit sides of bowl. Beat until mixture is glossy with smooth peaks, 10 to 15 minutes. Gently fold in almond flour mixture in thirds, being careful not to deflate egg whites.
• Spoon mixture into a piping bag fitted with a medium round tip (Wilton #12). Pipe batter into drawn circles on prepared baking sheet. Tap pans vigorously on counter 4 to 5 times to release air bubbles. Let stand at room temperature until macarons form a skin, 45 to 60 minutes. (Macarons should feel dry to the touch and not stick to the finger.)
• Preheat oven to 280°.
• Bake until macarons are firm to the touch, 18 to 20 minutes, rotating pans halfway through baking. Let cool completely on pans.
• Transfer macarons to an airtight container with layers separated by wax paper. Refrigerate until ready to serve.
• Place Fruity & Floral Filling in a piping bag fitted with a medium round tip (Wilton #10). Pipe approximately ½ teaspoon filling onto flat side of 36 macarons. Place remaining macarons, flat side down, on top of filling. Lightly push down so filling spreads to edges. Serve immediately.

We used Beanilla Lavender Flavoring and Wilton Gel Icing Colors in Violet.

MAKE-AHEAD TIP: *Wrap unfilled macarons in plastic wrap in groups to prevent crushing or breaking. Transfer to airtight containers. Refrigerate for up to 2 days until needed or freeze for up to 1 month. Let come to room temperature before filling and serving.*

Fruity & Floral Filling
MAKES APPROXIMATELY 1 CUP

A buttercream blended with mango-peach preserves and lavender flavoring can be used for filling a number of treats.

½ cup unsalted butter, softened
½ cup confectioners' sugar
¼ cup mango-peach preserves
¼ teaspoon food-grade lavender flavoring*

• In a large bowl, beat together butter and sugar with a mixer at medium speed until creamy, 3 to 4 minutes. Beat in preserves and lavender flavoring.

We used Beanilla Lavender Flavoring.

Mini Carrot Cakes
MAKES 35

While we've lightened the batter of these cakes by using olive oil instead of butter, the frosting is as rich and decadent as ever, as are the pretty pink-and-white squares of white chocolate.

3 large eggs, room temperature
1¼ cups granulated sugar
¼ cup plus 2 tablespoons extra-virgin olive oil
½ teaspoon vanilla extract
1 cup plus 2 tablespoons all-purpose flour
1 teaspoon baking soda
1 teaspoon ground cinnamon
¼ teaspoon ground allspice
¼ teaspoon ground nutmeg
¼ teaspoon fine sea salt
½ (10-ounce) bag shredded carrots
½ cup chopped walnuts, toasted
½ cup golden raisins (sultanas)
½ (11-ounce) bag white chocolate chips
Pink food coloring
Honeyed Cream Cheese Frosting (recipe follows)

• Preheat oven to 375°. Spray a 12½x9-inch rimmed sheet pan with baking spray with flour and line pan with parchment paper.
• In the bowl of a stand mixer fitted with whisk attachment, beat together eggs and sugar at medium-high speed until pale yellow and fluffy, approximately 3 minutes. Reduce mixer speed to medium-low. Add oil and vanilla extract in a slow, steady stream, beating until combined, 3 to 5 minutes.

• In a medium bowl, whisk together flour, baking soda, cinnamon, allspice, nutmeg, and salt. Using a rubber spatula, fold flour mixture into egg mixture just until combined. Fold in carrots, walnuts, and raisins. Using an offset spatula, spread batter into prepared sheet pan.
• Bake until a wooden pick inserted in center comes out clean, 25 to 35 minutes. Let cool completely in pan on a wire rack.
• Meanwhile, in a medium microwave-safe bowl, microwave white chocolate chips on high in 30-second intervals, stirring between each, until melted and smooth.
• In a small bowl, stir together ½ cup melted white chocolate and desired amount of pink food coloring until combined. Transfer pink chocolate to a piping bag fitted with a round tip (Wilton #4).
• Using an offset spatula, spread remaining melted white chocolate to a ⅛-inch thickness onto a nonstick baking mat. Pipe vertical lines of pink chocolate ¼ inch apart onto white chocolate. Beginning at top left corner, use a wooden pick to drag chocolate from left to right, then right to left, changing directions as you move down white chocolate. Let chocolate set slightly. Using a 1½-inch square cutter, cut 35 chocolate squares. Let chocolate set completely.
• Run a paring knife around edges of pan to loosen cake. Invert pan to release cake onto a cutting surface. Discard parchment paper. Using a sharp knife, trim and discard ½ inch from cake edges, and cut cake into 1½-inch squares, wiping knife clean between each cut. Spread 1 tablespoon Honeyed Cream Cheese Frosting on top of each square. Place a chocolate square on top of each frosted cake square. Serve immediately.

Honeyed Cream Cheese Frosting
MAKES 2¼ CUPS

Cream cheese frosting is a popular topping for carrot cake. Add some honey to it for an increased, natural source of sweetness.

1½ (8-ounce) packages cream cheese, softened
4 ounces mascarpone cheese
1½ tablespoons honey
1½ cups confectioners' sugar

• In a large bowl, beat together cream cheese, mascarpone cheese, and honey with a mixer at medium speed until creamy, 3 to 4 minutes, stopping to scrape sides of bowl. Reduce mixer speed to low. Gradually add confectioners' sugar, beating just until combined.

Pavlovas with Vanilla Bean Mousse

MAKES 24

Pavlovas are delectable meringue treats that hold a variety of fillings. For this recipe, the nest shape perfectly contains a layer of Vanilla Bean Mousse and assorted fresh seasonal fruit.

4 large egg whites, room temperature
½ teaspoon vanilla extract
¼ teaspoon cream of tartar
¾ cup granulated sugar
Vanilla Bean Mousse (recipe follows)
Assorted fresh seasonal fruit*
1 tablespoon honey
Garnish: finely chopped dried rose petals

• Preheat oven to 200°. Line 2 rimmed baking sheets with parchment paper. Using a pencil, draw 24 (2-inch) circles onto each parchment sheet; turn parchment over.
• In the bowl of a stand mixer fitted with the whisk attachment, beat together egg whites, vanilla extract, and cream of tartar at medium speed until foamy. Add sugar, 1 tablespoon at a time, beating at high speed until stiff peaks form, 5 to 7 minutes. Transfer meringue mixture to a piping bag fitted with a medium open-star tip (Ateco #822).
• Starting in the center of each drawn circle, pipe concentric circles of meringue mixture outward until each circle is filled. (Turn to page 130 for step-by-step how-to photographs.) Pipe 1 to 2 extra layers onto perimeters to

form a rim around the edge of each circle. In the margins of parchment, pipe small star shapes to use for garnish, if desired.
• Bake until pavlovas are set and dry, approximately 2 hours. Turn oven off, and let meringues stand in oven with door closed for 1 hour. (This helps meringues continue to dry and form a crispy shell.) Store at room temperature in an airtight container with layers separated with wax paper until needed.
• Just before serving, divide Vanilla Bean Mousse among meringues (pavlovas). Top with fresh fruit. Brush fruit with honey. Place a meringue star atop fruit.
• Garnish with dried rose petals, if desired. Serve immediately.

We used red grapes, pomegranate arils, and fresh figs.

Vanilla Bean Mousse

MAKES ¾ CUP

Mildly sweet mascarpone allows the sweetness of honey and vanilla bean to shine.

6 ounces mascarpone
½ tablespoon honey
⅛ teaspoon vanilla bean paste

• In a medium bowl, whisk together mascarpone, honey, and vanilla bean paste until combined. Use immediately.

Ginger-Rooibos Crème Brûlée Tartlets

MAKES 15

Instead of serving in ramekins, these tea-infused crème brûlée bites are perched on piecrust rounds and offer the consistency of the favored dessert but in tiny tartlet form.

½ (14.1-ounce) package refrigerated piecrust dough
  (1 sheet)
1 large egg
¾ cup plus 1 tablespoon heavy whipping cream, divided
2 tablespoons loose-leaf lemon-ginger rooibos*
4 large egg yolks, room temperature
¼ cup granulated sugar
¾ teaspoon freshly grated gingerroot
½ teaspoon vanilla bean paste**
2 tablespoons ginger cane sugar
Garnish: fresh lemon zest

• Preheat oven to 400°. Line a rimmed baking sheet with parchment paper.
• On a lightly floured surface, unroll dough. Using a 2-inch fluted round cutter, cut 15 rounds from dough. Place dough rounds on prepared baking sheet. Using a fork, prick several holes on surface of dough rounds. Freeze for 10 minutes.
• In a small bowl, whisk together egg and 1 tablespoon cream. Brush egg mixture onto dough rounds.
• Bake until edges of rounds are golden brown, 10 to 12 minutes. Let cool completely on a wire rack. Store crust rounds in an airtight container at room temperature until needed, up to 2 days.
• Reduce oven temperature to 300°. Place a 15-well mini Bundt cake silicone mold*** on a rimmed baking sheet.
• In a small saucepan, bring remaining ¾ cup cream to a simmer over medium heat. Remove from heat. Add rooibos, stirring well. Let steep for 10 minutes.
• Strain cream mixture through a fine-mesh sieve into a medium bowl; discard rooibos. Add egg yolks, granulated sugar, ginger, and vanilla bean paste, stirring until smooth and well combined. Divide crème brûlée mixture among wells of prepared mold, filling each well to top. Pass flame of a kitchen torch over filled mold to release any air bubbles. Place baking sheet in oven. Pour ½ inch warm tap water around mold onto baking sheet.
• Bake until crèmes brûlées are set, 18 to 20 minutes. (When you lightly shake baking sheet, being careful not to spill hot water, the crèmes brûlées should not move in centers.) Let cool to room temperature. Pour water out of baking sheet. Place baking sheet with

silicone mold in the freezer for at least 3 hours.
• Place cane sugar in a shallow dish. Carefully remove crèmes brûlées from mold. Dip tops of crèmes brûlées in sugar, and place on baking sheet. Using a kitchen torch, toast sugar-coated tops. Using an offset spatula, place a crème brûlée onto each prepared crust round.
• Garnish with lemon zest, if desired. Serve immediately, or let crèmes brûlées come to room temperature.

We used Simpson & Vail Lemon Ginger Rooibos Tea, available at svtea.com or by calling 800-282-8327.
**If vanilla bean paste is not available, replace with an equal amount of pure vanilla extract.*
***We used Sunny Side Up Bakery Mini Bundt Cake Silicone Mold, available at hobbylobby.com.*

- Preheat oven to 325°. Line several rimmed baking sheets with parchment paper.
- In a large mixing bowl, beat together butter and granulated sugar with a mixer at medium speed until light and creamy. Add vanilla extract, beating until incorporated.
- In a medium bowl, combine flour and salt, whisking well. Add flour mixture to butter mixture, beating just until incorporated. Add chocolate chips, stirring to combine.
- Using a levered 1-teaspoon scoop, divide dough into portions. Roll dough portions into balls, and shape balls into crescents. Place crescents 2 inches apart on prepared baking sheets.
- Bake until firm and bottoms are golden brown, approximately 15 minutes. Let cool for 2 to 3 minutes.
- Coat warm cookies in confectioners' sugar, and place on wire cooling racks. Let cool completely. Store in an airtight container with layers separated by wax paper until ready to serve.
- Before serving, dust with any remaining confectioners' sugar, if desired.

Pine Nut Tartlets
MAKES 24

Pine nuts combined with sugar, honey, and vanilla extract create a perfect sweet filling for these baked tartlets. A whipped cream piped star makes a lovely and tasty garnish.

2 (14.1-ounce) packages refrigerated piecrust dough
  (4 sheets)
½ cup pine nuts, toasted
¾ cup granulated sugar
¼ cup unsalted butter, melted
¼ cup honey
2 large eggs, lightly beaten
2 tablespoons whole milk
1 tablespoon all-purpose flour
1 tablespoon cornmeal
1½ teaspoons distilled white vinegar
¼ teaspoon vanilla extract
⅛ teaspoon salt
Sweetened Whipped Cream (recipe on page 68)

- Preheat oven to 450°.
- Lightly spray 24 (2½-inch) tartlet pans with cooking spray.
- Using a 3-inch round cutter, cut 24 rounds from dough sheets. (See how-to on page 129.) Press dough rounds into tartlet pans, trimming excess as necessary. Using

Chocolate Chip Crescent Cookies
MAKES 58

Shaped into small crescent moons, these shortbread versions of classic chocolate chip cookies are hidden beneath a layer of confectioners' sugar.

1 cup unsalted butter, softened
½ cup granulated sugar
½ teaspoon vanilla extract
2 cups all-purpose flour
½ teaspoon fine sea salt
1 cup mini semisweet chocolate chips
2 cups confectioners' sugar

large end of a chopstick, press dough into indentations in sides of tartlet pans. Using a fork, prick bottoms of dough to prevent puffing. Place tartlet pans on rimmed baking sheets. Freeze for 15 minutes.
• Bake until tartlet shells are light golden brown, approximately 5 minutes. Let cool completely.
• Divide pine nuts evenly among cooled tartlet shells.
• In a large liquid-measuring cup, combine sugar, melted butter, honey, eggs, milk, flour, cornmeal, vinegar, vanilla extract, and salt, stirring until well blended. Divide mixture among prepared tartlet shells, filling no more than three-quarters full.
• Bake until filling is set, approximately 13 minutes. Let cool completely before carefully removing tartlets from pans.
• Just before serving, place Sweetened Whipped Cream in a piping bag fitted with a very large closed-star tip (Ateco #855). Holding piping bag perpendicular to tartlets, pipe a star onto each tartlet.

Earl Grey Truffles
MAKES 24

Steep classic Earl Grey tea in heavy whipping cream for the centers of these stylish candies made in gem-shaped molds.

¼ cup plus 1 tablespoon heavy whipping cream
10 tea bags Earl Grey black tea
1⅔ cups 60% chocolate chips
1½ cups 66% cacao semisweet chocolate baking wafers
Garnish: edible pearl shimmer dust

• In a small saucepan, heat cream to a simmer. Remove from heat. Add tea bags, and steep for 20 minutes. Remove tea bags, squeezing excess tea into cream mixture. Return pan to stove, and bring just to a boil over medium heat.
• Place chocolate chips in a large heatproof bowl. Pour cream over chocolate, stirring until a smooth ganache forms. Cover with plastic wrap, pressing down so plastic wrap touches surface of ganache, and let cool.
• In a large microwave-safe bowl, melt chocolate wafers in microwave oven in 30-second intervals, stirring between each interval, until chocolate is smooth. Pour melted chocolate into wells of 2 (12-well) silicone or plastic candy molds*. Turn molds over, emptying excess chocolate into a bowl to reserve. (Let chocolate drip out until outlines of bottom of molds are visible when turned over.) Let chocolate set slightly. Using a bench scraper,

remove excess chocolate. Let chocolate set completely, right side up.
• Transfer Earl Grey ganache to a piping bag fitted with a small round tip (Wilton #4). Pipe chocolate ganache into wells of prepared candy molds, filling each about three-fourths full. Freeze for 10 minutes.
• Gently reheat reserved melted chocolate until smooth, if necessary. Spread melted chocolate over molds to cover ganache and form bottoms. Using a bench scraper, remove excess chocolate from molds and bottoms of truffles. Freeze for 10 minutes.
• Remove truffles from molds. Using a sharp paring knife, trim and clean any rough edges.
• Garnish tops of truffles with shimmer dust, if desired.
• Store in an airtight container in a cool, dark place for up to 2 weeks.

We used Celebrate It Gemstone Silicone Candy Molds, available at Michaels, michaels.com.

Strawberry Tea Cakes
MAKES 12

Assembled in the wells of a miniature cheesecake pan, these dainty cakes are stunningly beautiful alternatives to serving guests a slice from a large two-layer cake.

½ cup unsalted butter, softened
1 cup granulated sugar
2 large eggs, room temperature
½ teaspoon vanilla extract
1⅓ cups all-purpose flour
1¼ teaspoons baking powder

¼ teaspoon fine sea salt
½ cup heavy whipping cream
3 cups (1 pound) small fresh strawberries, stemmed and cut into halves
Coconut Cream Filling (recipe follows)
Garnish: fanned fresh strawberry halves

• Preheat oven to 350°. Line bottom of a 9-inch round cake pan with parchment paper; spray with baking spray with flour.
• In a large bowl, beat together butter and sugar with a mixer at medium speed until fluffy, 3 to 4 minutes, stopping to scrape sides of bowl. Add eggs, one at a time, beating well after each addition. Add vanilla extract, beating until incorporated.
• In a medium bowl, whisk together flour, baking powder, and salt. With mixer at low speed, gradually add flour mixture to butter mixture alternately with cream, beginning and ending with flour mixture, beating just until combined after each addition. Spoon batter into prepared pan.
• Bake until a wooden pick inserted in center comes out clean, 30 to 35 minutes. Let cool in pan for 10 minutes. Remove from pan, and let cool completely on a wire rack.
• Using a tall, 2-inch round cutter, cut 12 rounds from cake, beginning ¼ inch from cake edge. Using a serrated knife in a gentle sawing motion, cut cake rounds in half horizontally, creating 24 even layers.
• Line each well of a 12-well removable-bottom miniature cheesecake pan with an 8x2-inch parchment-paper collar. (IMPORTANT: Tape each collar where ends overlap to ensure parchment does not expand when filling.) Place a cake round in each well. On top of each round in pan, arrange 4 strawberry halves vertically, cut side out, around edges of wells.
• Place Coconut Cream Filling in a piping bag fitted with a medium round tip (Wilton #10). Pipe filling into prepared wells, being careful to pipe between strawberries and to cover them with a ¼-inch layer. Top each with a remaining cake round. Cover pan well with plastic wrap. Refrigerate until chilled and set, 4 to 8 hours. Store remaining Coconut Cream Filling in a piping bag fitted with a large star tip (Wilton #1M), wrapped gently, in the refrigerator.
• Remove cakes from pan by gently lifting with parchment collar. Remove bottom discs and parchment collars. Pipe a rosette of the reserved Coconut Cream Filling on top of each cake. Garnish with fanned strawberry halves, if desired.
• Serve immediately, or place cakes in an airtight container, and refrigerate for a few hours until ready to serve.

Coconut Cream Filling
MAKES APPROXIMATELY 3 CUPS

Cream of coconut—a smooth, syrupy liquid made from the fresh fruit—and coconut extract infuse the tropical flavor into this decadent cream cheese filling.

2 (8-ounce) packages cream cheese, softened
½ cup confectioners' sugar, sifted
1 cup heavy whipping cream
¼ cup cream of coconut
¼ teaspoon coconut extract

• In a large bowl, beat cream cheese and confectioners' sugar with a mixer at medium speed until smooth, approximately 3 minutes, stopping to scrape sides of bowl with a rubber spatula. Add heavy cream, cream of coconut, and coconut extract, and beat until stiff peaks form, 2 to 3 minutes. Use immediately.

Key Lime Tartlets
MAKES 10

A classic summertime dessert is transformed into pretty tartlets topped with piped meringue that are perfect for afternoon tea.

1½ (14.1-ounce) packages refrigerated piecrust dough
  (3 sheets)
2 large eggs, divided
1¾ cups sweetened condensed milk
½ cup fresh Key lime juice
1 large egg white
¼ cup granulated sugar
Garnish: fresh lime zest

• Preheat oven to 400°. Line 2 rimmed baking sheets with parchment paper.
• On a lightly floured surface, unroll dough. Using a 4½-inch round cutter, cut 10 rounds from dough. (See how-to on page 129.) Transfer rounds to 10 (3¾-inch) fluted round removable-bottom tartlet pans. Using wide end of a chopstick, gently press dough into indentations in sides of pans. Using a fork, prick bottom of dough in tartlet pans 4 times. Place tartlet pans on prepared baking sheets. Freeze for 15 minutes.
• In a small bowl, lightly whisk 1 egg. Brush beaten egg onto tartlet shells (dough). Top each tartlet shell with a parchment paper square, letting ends extend over edges of pans. Add pie weights or dried beans.

• Bake until edges of tartlet shells are golden brown, 12 to 15 minutes. Let cool completely on a wire rack before carefully removing parchment and weights. Reduce oven temperature to 350°.
• In a medium bowl, whisk together condensed milk, lime juice, and remaining 1 egg until combined. Divide filling among prepared tartlet shells.
• Bake until filling is set, approximately 10 minutes. Let cool completely.
• In the top of a double boiler, whisk together egg white and sugar. Cook over simmering water, whisking constantly, until sugar dissolves. Remove from heat. With a mixer at high speed, beat mixture until glossy white and stiff peaks form, 3 to 5 minutes.
• Transfer meringue to a piping bag fitted with a small star tip (Wilton #16). Holding piping bag perpendicular to tartlets, pipe small drops of meringue onto tartlets. Using a small kitchen torch*, carefully brown meringue. Place tartlets in an airtight container, and refrigerate for up to a day.
• Before serving, carefully remove tartlets from pans.
• Garnish with lime zest, if desired.

If a kitchen torch is not available, meringue can be browned under a broiler, watching carefully to prevent burning.

- Turn out dough onto a lightly floured surface, and gently knead 3 to 4 times. Between 2 large parchment paper sheets, roll out dough to a ¼-inch thickness. Transfer dough with parchment to refrigerator. Refrigerate until set, at least 2 hours.
- Preheat oven to 325°. Line 2 baking sheets with parchment paper.
- In a small bowl, lightly whisk remaining 1 egg yolk. Using a 1½-inch round cutter dipped in flour, cut as many cookies as possible from dough, rerolling scraps as necessary. Brush edges of cookies with a thin layer of beaten egg, and roll edges in lemon-hibiscus sugar. Place cookies at least ½ inch apart on prepared baking sheets. Freeze until set, approximately 15 minutes.
- Bake, in batches, until bottom edges of cookies are golden, 11 to 13 minutes. Let cool completely on baking sheets on wire racks. Store at room temperature for up to a day in an airtight container with layers separated with parchment paper.

Available at etsy.com.

Hibiscus-Lemon Sablés
MAKES APPROXIMATELY 30

Sablés are a French rendition of shortbread cookies. The edges of these sweet treats are rolled in crushed lemon-hibiscus sugar cubes for lovely crunch and taste. Alternatively, replace the flavored sugar cubes with sugar you scent with lemon zest and dried organic hibiscus petals that you let sit overnight or until the sugar has absorbed the desired amount of fragrance.

½ cup unsalted butter, softened
½ cup granulated sugar
2 tablespoons plus 2 teaspoons confectioners' sugar
¼ teaspoon fine sea salt
½ teaspoon vanilla extract
2 large egg yolks, room temperature and divided
1¼ cups all-purpose flour
12 cubes lemon-hibiscus sugar cubes*, crushed

- In a large bowl, beat together butter, granulated sugar, confectioners' sugar, and salt with a mixer at medium speed until smooth, approximately 2 minutes. Add vanilla extract and 1 egg yolk, beating until combined, approximately 1 minute. Add flour, half at a time, beating just until combined after each addition.

Ginger Cakes with Rosy Apple Compote
MAKES 20

Infuse the batter of these cakes with spiced apple–flavored rooibos and candied ginger for a toothsome treat that evokes the flavors of the autumn season.

½ cup unsalted butter, softened
1 cup granulated sugar
2 large eggs
1 large egg yolk
¼ teaspoon vanilla extract
2 cups all-purpose flour
1 tablespoon finely chopped candied ginger
2 teaspoons baking powder
2 teaspoons ground ginger
½ teaspoon fine sea salt
¼ teaspoon ground allspice
½ cup steeped spiced apple–flavored rooibos*
Garnish: confectioners' sugar
Rosy Apple Compote (recipe follows)

- Preheat oven to 350°.
- Spray 20 wells of 2 (12-well) mini Bundt pans with baking spray with flour.
- In a large mixing bowl, combine butter and granulated sugar. Beat at high speed with a mixer until light and creamy, approximately 3 minutes. Add eggs and egg

yolk, one at a time, beating well after each addition. Add vanilla extract, stirring to incorporate.

• In a medium bowl, combine flour, candied ginger, baking powder, ground ginger, salt, and allspice, whisking well. Add flour mixture to butter mixture in thirds, alternately with rooibos, beginning and ending with flour mixture.

• Using a levered 3-tablespoon scoop, divide batter evenly among prepared wells of pans. Tap pans forcefully on counter several times to settle batter and to remove air bubbles.

• Bake cakes until edges are golden brown and a wooden pick inserted in the centers comes out clean, 13 to 15 minutes. Let cool in pans for 10 minutes. Transfer cakes to wire racks, and let cool completely.

• Just before serving, garnish cakes with a dusting of confectioners' sugar, if desired.

• Spoon Rosy Apple Compote into wells of cakes. Serve immediately.

We used 1 tablespoon Cinnamon Apple Rooibos Tea from Adagio Teas, adagio.com to 1 cup boiling water, and let it steep for 5 minutes before straining and discarding infused rooibos. Use ½ cup steeped rooibos in the cake batter and the remainder in the Rosy Apple Compote.

Rosy Apple Compote
MAKES 2 CUPS

A compote is simply pieces of fruit, such as apple, cooked in sugar, creating a syrupy mixture that is superb, especially when served over ice cream or a myriad of other sweets like our Ginger Cakes.

2 tablespoons unsalted butter
2½ cups finely diced Gala apple
¼ cup granulated sugar
½ cup steeped spiced apple–flavored rooibos*

• In a medium nonstick sauté pan, melt butter over medium-high heat. Add apple and sugar, stirring for 2 to 3 minutes. Add rooibos, and cover pan, reducing heat to medium-low. Cook until apple is tender, approximately 10 minutes, stirring occasionally.

• Using a slotted spoon, transfer apple pieces to a bowl.

• Increase heat to high, and cook remaining liquid until reduced and slightly thickened and syrupy. Add to apples, stirring to blend. Use immediately, or transfer to a covered container, and refrigerate for up to a day. Warm gently in a sauté pan before using.

*See note at left.

How-tos

Let these step-by-step photographs serve as your visual guide.

ROSETTE NAPKIN FOLD

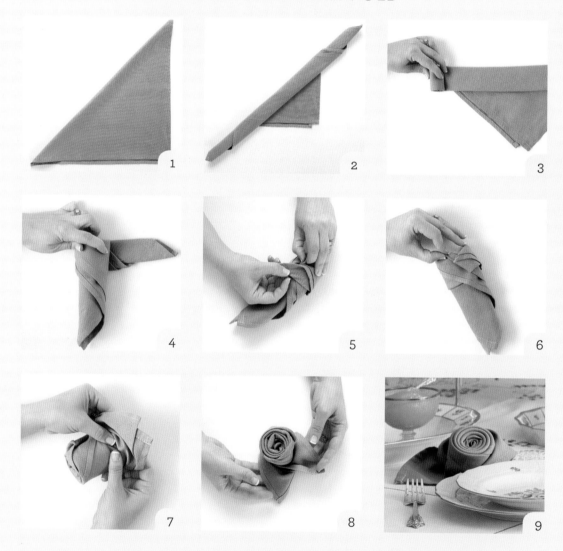

1) Fold a square napkin in half diagonally to create a triangle. 2) Beginning at longest edge, fold length of napkin over three times. Press, if desired. 3) Beginning at left end, roll napkin tightly. 4) Continue rolling napkin tightly. 5) Take hold of right end of napkin with one hand. 6) Tuck right end under top layer of napkin roll to secure end. 7) Grasp bottom points of napkin roll and fold up over sides of roll. 8) Gently pull ends of points to separate to resemble leaves. 9) Display as desired at place setting.

CHRISTMAS TREE NAPKIN FOLD

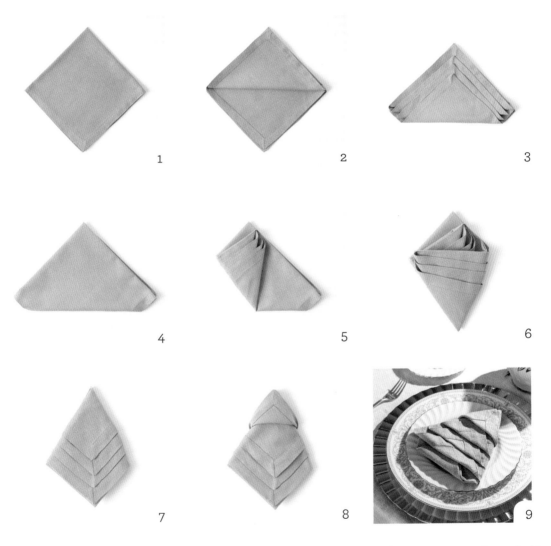

1) Fold a square napkin in half and then in half again to make a square. 2) With square set on point and with open edges at bottom, fold top layer up. 3) Fold remaining layers up individually in a staggered fashion. 4) Turn napkin over. 5) Fold over one-third of napkin. 6) Fold over opposite one-third of napkin. 7) Turn folded napkin over and orient as pictured. 8) Fold top layer up toward point. 9) Fold remaining layers up individually in a staggered fashion, tucking each point under the preceding layer, and fold shortest layer under.

TARTLET CRUST

1

Using a cutter, cut shapes from dough.

2

Press dough shapes into tartlet pans.

3

Trim excess dough.

4

Using the wide end of a chopstick, push dough into indentations of pan.

CUCUMBER FLOWER

1

Fold very thin slices of cucumber in half, and fold again into quarters.

2

Place on prepared canapés with point facing the center.

3

Add four more folded cucumber slices, letting them unfold slightly to resemble the petals of a flower.

PAVLOVAS

1) Line a baking sheet with parchment paper. Trace 2-inch circles onto parchment. Flip parchment paper over.

2) Working from the center outward, pipe concentric circles of meringue mixture until circle is filled.

3) Pipe 1 to 2 extra layers onto perimeters of rounds to form a rim around the edge of each meringue circle.

4) Repeat piping procedure to fill all traced circles. Bake according to recipe.

STRAWBERRY ROSETTE

1) Using a pairing knife, make 2 intersecting cuts in each strawberry, keeping the base intact.

2) On each quarter of the strawberry, make a small cut, angling the knife slightly inward.

Acknowledgments

EDITOR Lorna Reeves
ART DIRECTOR Cailyn Haynes
ASSOCIATE EDITOR Britt Crawford
SENIOR COPY EDITOR Rhonda Lee Lother
EDITORIAL ASSISTANT Katherine Ellis
SENIOR DIGITAL IMAGING SPECIALIST Delisa McDaniel
DIGITAL IMAGING SPECIALIST Clark Densmore

COVER

Photography by Stephanie Welbourne Steel
Styling by Melissa Sturdivant Smith
Recipe Development by Janet Lambert
Food Styling by Megan Lankford

Royal Copenhagen *Henriette* teapot, 11-inch oval serving platter, 14-inch oval serving platter, and medium vase, *Light Saxon Flower* mini creamer and sugar bowl; Herend *Golden Edge Newer* dinner plate, *Printemps* dessert/pie plate and flat cup and saucer set; Wallace Silver *Golden Grande Baroque* demitasse spoon, salad fork, modern hollow knife, and teaspoon from Replacements, Ltd.* Godinger *Dublin* crystal 3-tier serving rack from Bed, Bath & Beyond, *bedbathandbeyond.com.*

BE MY VALENTINE

Photography by John O'Hagan • Styling by Courtni Bodiford • Recipe Development by Janet Lambert • Food Styling by Megan Lankford

Pages 15–28: Royal Albert *Lavender Rose* teapot, salad plate, single egg cup, marmalade, large sandwich tray, and 3-tiered serving tray; Royal Albert *ROA8* creamer and open sugar bowl; Gorham Silver *Chantilly* new French hollow knife, salad fork, and teaspoon from Replacements, Ltd.* Aynsley *Hathaway* dinner plate; Royal Doulton *Adrian* footed cup and saucer set; Noritake *Perspective* pink glasses available for rent at Tea and Old Roses, 205-413-7753, *teaandoldroses.com.* Floral arrangement by Bronwyn Cardwell.

JOYOUS EASTER

Photography by John O'Hagan • Styling by Courtni Bodiford • Recipe Development by Janet Lambert • Food Styling by Kathleen Kanen

Pages 29–42: Royal Winton *Cheadle* teapot, Athena creamer, and open sugar bowl, *Clevedon* teapot, Norman creamer and open sugar bowl, and *Summertime* 2-tiered serving tray, 3-tiered serving tray, dinner plate, and handled cake plate; Royal Doulton *Easter Morn* footed cup and saucer set and salad plate; Gorham Silver *Rondo* demitasse spoon and *Strasbourg* new French hollow knife, salad fork, and teaspoon from Replacements, Ltd.* April Cornell tablecloth from HomeGoods, 800-888-0776, *homegoods.com.*

CELEBRATING MOTHERS

Photography by Stephanie Welbourne Steel
Styling by Melissa Sturdivant Smith
Recipe Development by Janet Lambert
Food Styling by Megan Lankford

Pages 43–54: Royal Copenhagen *Henriette* teapot, 11-inch oval serving platter, 14-inch oval serving platter, and medium vase, *Light Saxon Flower* handled cake plate, mini creamer and sugar bowl; Herend *Golden Edge Newer* dinner plate, *Printemps* dessert/pie plate and flat cup and saucer set; Anna Weatherley *Simply Anna Gold* 12-inch chop plate; Wallace Silver *Golden Grande Baroque* demitasse spoon, salad fork, modern hollow knife, and teaspoon from Replacements, Ltd.* Godinger *Dublin* crystal 3-tier serving rack from Bed, Bath & Beyond, *bedbathandbeyond.com.* Wrapping paper from Dogwood Hill and Wallpaper Boulevard.

CHERISHED THANKSGIVING

Photography by John O'Hagan • Styling by Courtni Bodiford • Recipe Development by Janet Lambert • Food Styling by Kathleen Kanen

Pages 55–68: Johnson Brothers *Devonshire Brown Multicolor* teapot, flat cup and saucer set, square salad plate, dinner plate, creamer, and sugar bowl; Spode *Delamere Brown* dinner plate; Oneida Silver *Cantata* modern solid knife, salad fork, and teaspoon from Replacements, Ltd.* Festival napkins in Paprika from Sferra, 732-225-6290, *sferra.com.* Tiered stands available for rent at Tea and Old Roses, 205-413-7753, *teaandoldroses.com.* Floral arrangement by No.5 Floral Design, 205-913-4841, *no5floraldesign.com.*

EVERGREEN CHRISTMAS

Photography by Mac Jamieson
Styling by Courtni Bodiford and Lily Simpson
Recipe Development by Janet Lambert
Food Styling by Kellie Kelley

Pages 69–80: Sudlow Burslem (pattern unknown) teapot; Royal Worcester *Allegro* dinner plate; Minton *Cheviot Green* salad plate, bread and butter plate, creamer, sugar, flat cup and saucer set, dinner plates for tiered stand, and small oval sugar for creamer and sugar; Rogers *First Love* flatware; Myott *Old Silver Lustre* 3-part server; Royal Albert *Antoinette* round platter; gold chargers and tiered stand available for rent at Tea and Old Roses, 205-413-7753, *teaandoldroses.com.* Jadeite Green buffet napkins from World Market, 877-967-5362, *worldmarket.com.* Centerpiece by No.5 Floral Design, 205-913-4841, *no5floraldesign.com.*

SCONES

Page 83: Lenox *Vintage Jewel* footed cup and saucer set and 2-tiered server from Lenox, 800-223-4311, *lenox.com.* Silver condiment bowls from World Market, 877-967-5362, *worldmarket.com.* Page 84: Noritake *Crestwood Cobalt Platinum* bread and butter plate and teapot from Replacements, Ltd.* Page 85: Royal Copenhagen *Golden Basket* bread and butter plate from Replacements, Ltd.* Page 86: Bawo & Dotter *BWD31* footed cup and saucer set and bread and butter plate from Replacements, Ltd.* Page 87: Kashima *Christmas Holly* 10-inch star-shape platter from Replacements, Ltd.* Page 88: Royal Doulton *Rondo* bread and butter plate from Replacements, Ltd.* Page 89: Lenox *Holiday Tartan* serving plate with handle from Replacements, Ltd.* Page 91: Fostoria *June Topaz* platter from Replacements, Ltd.* Page 92: Wedgwood *Golden Grosgrain* 5-piece place setting from Replacements, Ltd.* Page 93:

Wedgwood *Amherst* bread and butter plate, salad plate, and dinner plate; Westmoreland Silver *George & Martha Washington* butter spreader from Replacements, Ltd.* Page 94: Two-tiered stand from World Market, 877-967-5362, *worldmarket.com.* Page 95: Bernardaud *Le Gobelet du Roy* bread and butter plate from Bernardaud, 212-371-4300, *bernardaud.com.* Page 96: Haviland *Oasis* dinner plate, teacup, and saucer from Bromberg's, 205-871-3276, *brombergs.com.* Hutschenreuther *Baroness Gold* salad plate from Replacements, Ltd.* Vintage Royal Crown (Japan) *Lusterware 905* bread and butter plate from private collection.

SAVORIES

Page 99: Shelley *Hedgerow* salad plate from Replacements, Ltd.* Page 100: Lenox *Opal Innocence Scroll Gold* footed cup and saucer set and oval platter, 800-223-4311, *lenox.com.* Page 101: Herend *Golden Edge* round tray with handles and *Golden Trellis* teacup and tea saucer from Herend, 800-643-7363, *herendusa.com.* Page 103: Herend *Winter Shimmer* sandwich tray from Herend, 800-643-7363, *herendusa.com.* Page 104: Lenox *Pearl Platinum* creamer from Lenox, 800-223-4311, *lenox.com.* Page 105: Lenox *Tyler* 13-inch oval serving platter from Replacements, Ltd.* Page 106: Lenox *Hancock* accent plate from Replacements, Ltd.* Page 107: Royal Doulton *Rondo* oval platter from Replacements, Ltd.* Page 108: Bernardaud *Le Gobelet du Roy* square tray from Bernardaud, 212-371-4300, *bernardaud.com.* Oneida *Golden Michelangelo* flatware from Oneida, 888-263-7195, *oneida.com.* Page 109: Hutschenreuther *Revere* platter from Replacements, Ltd.* Page 110: Royal Doulton *Rondo* oval platter from Replacements, Ltd.*

SWEETS

Page 115: Reed & Barton silver 2-tier stand from Bromberg's, 205-871-3276, *brombergs.com.* Page 117: Bernardaud *Le Gobelet du Roy* salad plate from Bernardaud, 212-371-4300, *bernardaud.com.* Page 120: Royal Copenhagen *Golden Basket* pickle dish and teacup and saucer set from Replacements, Ltd.* Page 121: Noritake *Crestwood Cobalt Platinum* 11-inch oval serving platter from Replacements, Ltd.* Page 122: Annieglass *Ruffle Gold* small oval bowl from Bromberg's, 205-871-3276, *brombergs.com.* Lenox *Hancock* footed cup and saucer set from Replacements, Ltd.* Pages 123–125: Laura Ashley *Blueprint Collectables* 3-tiered stand from The London Merchant, 314-323-6463, *thelondonmerchant.com.* Page 126: Herend *Livia* teacup and saucer from Herend, 800-643-7363, *herendusa.com.*

BACK COVER

Reed & Barton silver 2-tier stand from Bromberg's, 205-871-3276, *brombergs.com.*

*Replacements, Ltd., 800-737-5223, replacements.com

EDITOR'S NOTE: Items not listed are from private collections, and no manufacturer/pattern information is available.

Recipe Index

*EDITOR'S NOTE: Recipes listed in italics
are gluten-free, provided gluten-free versions
of processed ingredients (such as condiments
and extracts) are used.*